Out of the Tunnel

Out of the Tunnel

Rachel North

First published in Great Britain in 2007 by Friday Books
An imprint of The Friday Project Limited
83 Victoria Street, London SW1H 0HW
www.thefridayproject.co.uk
www.fridaybooks.co.uk

Text © Rachel North 2007 All rights reserved

ISBN – 13   978-1-905548-75-0

British Library Cataloguing in Publication Data

A catalogue record for this book is available from the British
Library

Cover and internal design by Snowbooks Design

Author photograph © Ian Brodie
ibrodiephoto.com

Upper cover image © STEPHEN HIRD/Reuters/Corbis
Lower cover image © MIKE FINN-KELCEY/ Reuters/Corbis

Printed by MPG Books Ltd, Bodmin, Cornwall

The Publisher's policy is to use paper manufactured from sustainable
sources.

In the terror of 7th July Rachel North found her own capacity for courage and discovered that she had extraordinary gifts as a writer, not the least of which is her powerful honesty.

Fergal Keane

ACKNOWLEDGEMENTS

I WOULD LIKE TO EXPRESS my grateful thanks to the following.

My wonderful husband, who means everything to me.

My family and friends, who have given me so much love.

My fellow passengers, the men and women of King's Cross United, who continue to inspire me.

My blog readers, who have given me so much support.

London Underground staff, the staff of the emergency services, especially London Ambulance Service, the Metropolitan Police and the British Transport Police, London Fire Brigade and the medical staff and passers-by who responded bravely and compassionately on July 7 2005.

Especially Tom and Ray, Steve and Gerard, and David.

Charlotte Street NHS Traumatic Stress Clinic.

July 7 Assistance Centre

Jane Corrigan, Ann Brebner, David Hanley and Paul Davidson, ex-Operation Sapphire (the Metropolitan Police Sexual Offences Investigation team) and all their colleagues who worked on the rape case in 2002.

Fergal Keane, Gary Duffy, and the BBC.

The Friday Project

David Godwin Associates
Urban 75
Out of the Tunnel is dedicated to all those who have walked in darkness, and to those who walk with them into the light.

CHAPTER ONE

July morning, July night

THURSDAY 7TH JULY 2005 BEGAN with me waking curled into my boyfriend J's back, both of us bone-tired, me from sleeplessness, and he from having worked until the early hours at his law firm. We ignored the alarm, wordlessly signalling our disobedience to it by sliding deeper under the duvet. Another fifteen minutes of sweet drowsy warmth, scent of his hair; let me lie here longer, safe in my beloved's arms. But no, I was running late, and today was an important day, one I had been waiting for. I climbed out of bed, showered, fed the goldfish and Miff the fat tabby cat, and ran about the flat with wet hair, dithering over what to wear, because I had a big presentation to give that afternoon. Settled on my new black trouser suit, black and white linen top, favourite red leather cork-heeled platform sandals. No time for breakfast, though I gulped the tepid tea I had made for J. I did a twirl for him. He said I looked lovely, though he wasn't wearing his glasses. He looked shattered, still lying on the sofa of our North London flat, still in his dressing gown, face creased with exhaustion. We kissed, hard, then softly, and he wished me good luck. I didn't know then how much luck I would need that day.

Then I was striding through the grey morning streets, smelling the tang of rain in the air, heading for the kiosk at Finsbury Park station to buy *Marie Claire* magazine before boarding the train to work at my new advertising job in the West End. The magazine, published that day, contained a story about me, and I was nervous, anxious, excited to read it. I had given the interview months ago. I bought a newspaper, and the magazine, which had a free pair of sunglasses attached to it. I scanned the cover; it featured Elizabeth Hurley in bikini pants and a see-through kaftan with her nipples airbrushed out. My piece was not mentioned in the cover lines. It was not, after all, a very unusual or unique story.

The newspaper's triumphant headline was 'One Sweet Word: London' – the news of the Olympic celebrations yesterday as we had been told it would host the Games in 2012. I paid at the kiosk, and hurried down the stairs, turned right to the Piccadilly line platform, juggling my handbag, newspaper, magazine, the reams of unravelling plastic that the magazine was wrapped in, the blister-packed free sunglasses, moving with the practised ease of the long-term commuter through the crush of people.

I'd waited a long time to read this article. Dammit, there was nowhere to sit down and see what it said. I moved further up the platform, right to the end of the train. Stood where the first carriage stops, it was sometimes easier to get on there. I knew that there was no hope of getting a seat to work, not today.

I flicked my gaze up to the electronic train announcement board. Delays. The Piccadilly line, which normally runs a train every minute or so at rush hour, was running a terrible service, with trains every seven or eight minutes. 'Fire at Caledonian Road,' said the tannoy. 'There's so many flipping people trying to get onto the platform, they're still all crowded up the stairs,' said the woman in front of me to her friend. 'If it gets any more crowded they're going to have to close the station.' Her friend sighed, and swore. I briefly contemplated shoving my way back down the platform and taking the other train, but there were hundreds of people going the other way, and for all I knew, it was just as bad on the Victoria line.

It had gone half past eight. I was going to be late; we all were. People were huffing and sighing, irritated, the euphoria or shock of London winning the Olympic hosting bid on their newspaper pages diminished by the chaos of yet another fight to get to work on time on London's creakingly overstretched public transport system. A man next to me remarked to nobody in particular, 'How the bloody hell are we going to manage the Olympics when we can't even run the trains on time?' He was breaking the 'Don't Talk To Strangers' rule of the London Underground user so I ignored him. So did everyone else. I spied a space on the platform bench behind me. I sat down quickly, opened the magazine, scanned the contents page.

There it was, the article, told in the first person, though I wasn't allowed to write it up myself. There was my picture, partially obscured to protect my identity, as is usual with this sort of story. A few hundred words on glossy paper, swimming in front of me as my eyes teared up, and my heart started to beat faster. The platform, the crush of people, and the noise of the late train finally arriving faded away, as I started to read the story of my almost-death.

It was hard to read, because as I read it, I was reliving it all again. My heart was beating faster, and my breathing was shallow. I started a clammy sweat. I needed to compose myself, needed to get on the train, to make it into work and sit at my desk normally, without this embarrassing trembling reaction. I glanced up, concentrating on getting my breathing back to normal. Another train had just pulled in, and people were pushing themselves onto it. I could have squeezed on too, but I was worried that I was now in the early stages of a panic attack, and so I stayed on the bench. The tube doors hissed closed. The train pulled away. I got up, and moved towards the edge of the platform, ready for the next train. I knew I had to get on it, however crowded it might have been. I was going to be very late, and I had been in my job only six weeks. I was still on probation. I didn't want to get into trouble.

When the next tube came along, I was ready. I started to get on at the middle set of doors of the first carriage. I put my foot on the train, but at the last second I stepped back and decided to go a few metres further up, to board at the first set of doors, the very front of the train, where I thought I might have a little more space. I wanted to read that article again, more calmly this time. I wanted to get the fear and adrenaline out of my system, and to try instead to feel the pride, the pleasure that I'd survived. Because I was proud of it; proud that I was still here to tell my story, proud that the man who attacked me was now locked up, and couldn't hurt anyone else. I got onto the train and stood by the yellow pole in the centre of the standing area by the first set of doors. I held the pole with my right hand, my new blue handbag over my left shoulder, newspaper now shoved into the bag, holding the folded magazine in my left hand, worrying whether anyone else would read it over my shoulder and recognise me in the accompanying photo. But of course they wouldn't, nobody makes eye contact with their fellow passengers or speaks to them on the London Underground. It is the only way to maintain your composure in such crowded conditions, to pretend that all the other people don't exist.

We were off. This time it was easier for me to read my story. The train stopped at Arsenal, Holloway Road, Caledonian Road, with more and more people getting on at each stop. *This is the most crowded train I have ever been on,* I thought, *in over a dozen years of making this journey in from North London on the Piccadilly line. I bet I could lift my feet up off the floor and not fall over; I am wedged in so tight.*

Now we were at King's Cross, the doors slid open, people were pushing to get out, people were pushing to get in, I was being pushed away from the pole, back towards the centre of the carriage, I looked out through the open doors at the crowds. *My God, the platform is heaving here, six- or seven-deep, with fed-up commuters, all trying to stuff themselves into this delayed train. There is no way any more people can fit into this carriage, but still they come. I can't wait to escape from this sweating, irritable crush of humanity.*

Somewhere behind me, pushing onto my carriage, boarding

through the middle set of doors, unremarkable among all the commuters, was a young Jamaican-born British man with a rucksack. His rucksack contained ten pounds of explosives. He had travelled to London, rising early, leaving his pregnant wife and baby to join three friends at Luton station. The group of men had said goodbye to each other, hugged each other, happy, almost euphoric as they split up to continue their journeys. July 7th was a special day for this man and his friends. They had chosen to leave this world and to enter Paradise. And Germaine Lindsay, nineteen years old, the man climbing through the doors, pushing onto the train with the rest of the crowd, had chosen this rush-hour morning at King's Cross station, this train, and this carriage to die.

I didn't know this, of course; none of us knew what was about to happen, then. Maybe, somewhere there was a whisper of intelligence on the plot; maybe someone official came across this young man and assessed him as a low risk, made the judgement that he was no one worthy of special attention. Perhaps there were warnings somewhere, clues about what he and his friends wanted to do. A file on him, intelligence chatter, rumours, emails, a history of looking at the wrong websites, watching the wrong DVDs, talking to the wrong people... Something that could have warned us of the bomb in his bag and the hatred in his heart and the chaos and carnage he was moments away from unleashing. Whatever was known, it wasn't enough to stop him, and so he, like hundreds of others, was on board this overcrowded train.

The driver waited at King's Cross for several minutes, longer than usual, to allow as many people to scramble off and push on as possible. People who didn't make it and who were left on the platform looked angrily through the windows at us as the doors closed. The platform tannoy warned: 'This train is about to depart.'

Twenty-six people, and the bomber, had a few minutes left to live.

I found that I was crushed against another young woman. For a moment we were locked chest to chest in an intimate hug. We apologised to each other. My heart was beating fast and my body was still in a state of adrenalised fight-or-flight readiness, but there was nowhere to flee to. The irritation in the air was palpable, people uncomfortably pressed into each other, backs, elbows, bags, rucksacks.

The last person to board was a smiling black woman who was giggling in disbelief at the crush as she squeezed her curvaceous figure through the closing doors. Her warm humour defused the tension. The train started to move. I took a deep breath. Three more stops to go. I tried to compose myself for a busy day at work. I unclenched my fists. It was impossible to read anymore, all I could do was lift up my head and concentrate on breathing in and out to fight the claustrophobia, and read the adverts on the walls of the train.

And then I felt rather than heard an explosion; it was as if I had been punched violently in both ears. The world went as black as if I had been plunged deep underwater. Everything had changed in a heartbeat. And the thought flashed through me. 'Not again. Not bloody again.'

IT WAS ALMOST EXACTLY THREE years since the early hours of Friday 17 July 2002, when I had forced my way out of my North London flat, naked and covered in blood, with my hands bound behind my back and a wire noose around my neck, screaming as I threw my body across the bonnet of a police car.

The previous twenty-four hours had been normal enough. I had taken the tube to work in an advertising department office in South London near the Thames South Bank. It was a sweltering blue day. By lunchtime I had already been to three meetings in the West End, and the clothes I had picked out that morning to wear to work were limp and creased from hurrying about London using public transport. I had another important meeting in Victoria at 2pm, so I set off early and bought a cheap black cotton skirt and blouse in my lunch break at Victoria station shopping centre on the way to meet the client. Arriving at the client's offices, I changed into my new clothes in the loo, powdered my shining face and tied back my hair into a ponytail, changing myself into a fresher, cooler business proposition. But the meeting was not a success because the presentation I had prepared would not load and play properly on my laptop. And I had forgotten the hard copy. I talked around the ideas instead, promised to send over a copy of the presentation as soon as I got back to the office, but the opportunity had gone and we both knew it. I headed back to my desk, irritated with myself.

I spent the afternoon writing up another proposal for a meeting tomorrow, occasionally looking out of the window at the boats moving up and down the sparkling river, the big wheel of the London Eye turning slowly, the tourists sauntering in the glorious sun. In the office, phones rang constantly, many of them for absent colleagues which meant taking endless messages. I cursed the fact that I had no lunch meeting today.

Then I could have been out of the office, lingering over coffee at an outside table, instead of squinting at a proposed media schedule for a pitch we were unlikely to win. Half the bloody office seemed to be on holiday, I wished I was too. Emails arrived every five minutes, my boss wandered over to my desk to badger me about a meeting he wanted me to organise for next week, and I could feel my jaw tightening as I pushed my damp hair out of my eyes. I worked on the 24th floor of a 1970s tower block, and the air conditioning didn't work.

By 6pm I was gritting my teeth with stress. I couldn't face another sweaty tube journey home, not immediately, so I picked up my swimsuit which I kept under the desk in a plastic bag. As I stepped out of the office a warm breeze lifted my hair and the evening sun shone on my face. I walked to my gym, looking forward to plunging my body into cool water. There was an aqua-aerobics class about to start, so I joined about a dozen pink-cheeked women as we wallowed and splashed, kicked and pushed resistance floats while an instructor barked at us from the poolside over the blare of pop music. It was surprisingly hard work and afterwards, towelling myself dry, I realised I was starving. There hadn't been time for lunch. I left the gym and headed for a sushi bar opposite, treating myself to a few delicate slices of ballet-slipper-pink salmon, some warm rice, eye-watering wasabi stirred into salty soy sauce, vinegared seaweed and cucumber slices sprinkled with sesame seeds, and some green tea. I called a few girlfriends on my mobile, to see who was up for a glass of wine by the riverside. Everybody I called was just leaving for home, or not picking up. I thought about going back to the pub by my office, where some of my colleagues would be standing by the bar with pints of super-chilled lager, but I couldn't face any more work talk. I called my sister. She was delighted to hear from me.

'Oh brilliant, are you about? Ben's got tickets for that cool Polish bar in Southwark; they're having a third birthday party. There's a band, free drinks, come down, he knows all the bar staff,' she told me.

I got the tube from Waterloo and headed over. Anna and Ben, her boyfriend of the moment, were waiting for me in a pub called The Ring, by Southwark tube station. Ben had a large vodka and cranberry juice on the table for me, Anna looked glamorous in a backless gold halter-neck top. My long black skirt, flat sandals and high-necked black blouse looked dowdy in comparison, my makeup minimal after my swim. I borrowed some lip gloss from Anna, undid a few buttons, and we walked round the corner to the party. The bar was noisy and crowded, a band was playing Motown hits and I was introduced to a few of Ben's friends while a glass of vodka and spiced pear juice was thrust into my hand. Anna and I went to the cloakroom to drop off my wet swimming kit and her jacket. Then we stood near the band, jigging from foot to foot, watching the crowd, and catching up on the week's events. It was too loud to hear each other, so we came back to the bar, where Ben handed me another drink and introduced me to some more people. I put the drink on the bar; I didn't like it. It was warm, too sweet, and left my tongue feeling furred. The barman noticed.

'Don't like it? Want a shot instead?'

I hesitated, but Ben and his friend by my side accepted eagerly. This was a Polish bar after all, vodka shots its speciality. I used to work in Poland; I had spent a year before university teaching blind children in a convent school in a forest outside Warsaw. 'Have you got *Zubrowka*, bison grass vodka?' I asked, in Polish, experimentally, and the barman smiled and poured us all a cold glass. '*Na zdrowie*', I said, 'cheers' and we toasted the bar's success the Polish way. Eyes meet, and down in one.

I looked over at my sister, who was explaining about my year in Poland to the group around her. More people came to the bar and stood next to me; the barman began pouring more shots, telling me that Laski, the school where I had worked, was 'a special place', that it was very good that I had worked there. We talked about the Polish prime minister, whom I had surprised once, wandering without his minders in the garden outside the rooms I shared with another volunteer when I worked at Laski. The barman raised the bottle to us, as we all knocked back a second shot. 'To the children of Laski!' Then he immediately poured us a third.

I was feeling woozy with tiredness now, I had not eaten very much, and I had drunk too much alcohol far too quickly after exercising and running about all day. The three vodka shots, plus the drink in the pub before were giving me a headache, a tight band gripping my skull. J and I had rowed the night before; I was angry that I had seen so little of him, as night after night his law firm had kept him working late on a deal. I had barely seen him all week, and he had been working weekends. I walked away from the group at the bar to a quieter corner and called him, asking if he could join me and my sister. 'Just for an hour or so, just give yourself a break, honey, I need to see you,' I pleaded, but he said tightly, that he could not get away.

I felt a flash of disappointed anger. I looked down at my chipped toenail polish in my frumpy sandals. The evening had soured. As the veins throbbed in my temples, I decided to leave the party, the live band, the dancing, and the laughing crowds. I kissed my sister good night and told her that I was heading for home. She asked me to stay longer, stay over, but I thought of the next day's meetings, the unfinished pitch, the too-long list of things I had to do, and I sighed, and said no. I collected my bag with my wet swimming things from the cloakroom attendant, and stepped outside into the cool of the evening air. Dammit, now I realised I was drunk.

I thought briefly about going back into the bar, staying with Anna after all, but I couldn't face it. My headache was feeling better for the fresh air, and if I went now, I could avoid the crowds on the tube at pub-closing time. I wove my way to Southwark tube station, asked a London Underground staff member which platform I needed, and got onto the train which was pulling in. My head was pounding, so I closed my eyes against the bright lights of the carriage – and fell asleep almost at once. I woke, feeling disoriented after what felt like a few minutes. This wasn't right. I was at Stratford station, not Wood Green, not Green Park. The man at Southwark had told me the wrong train. Now I was miles from home, dazed with tiredness and vodka and facing another long journey before I could get into my bed. Swearing under my breath, I walked along the station platform, asking if there were any cabs. Someone told me where they might be found. There was one in the car park, dropping somebody off. The driver looked at me. 'I'm finished for the night, love. Where do you want to go?'

I told him Wood Green. He rolled his eyes. 'Okay. Hop in.'

I lolled in the back, closing my eyes again, wishing I was home, nauseous with pain and alcohol. My eyelids felt gritty and my mouth tasted bitter. The journey home seemed to take forever. I wondered if J would be at home when I got back. The cab stopped yet again at a red traffic light, near to home. There was no other traffic on the roads. I looked at the ticking meter. I had a £20 note in my purse, and the meter read £19.60. I decided to walk the last five minutes back to my flat, thinking the night air would help to clear my head and my nausea. I handed the note over to the driver, and got out.

The street was quiet, though in the distance I could hear a siren, and birdsong from a tree next to a bright streetlight. Nobody else was walking. It was about half-past midnight, the pubs had closed and the tubes had stopped running. I walked slowly, breathing deeply, thinking only of my headache, how stupid I had been to accept the free shots and down them in one, when I had work the next day. I did not notice whether anyone was following me. I did not think of any danger. I felt safe, walking the familiar way home that I had walked every day for four years. I left the main road, walked past the bus depot, through the well-lit council car park, full of CCTV cameras, past the hut which was the local minicab drivers' office, hearing the sound of Turkish music playing from their radio. Turned right into a well-lit residential street; nearly home now. I could see my flat as I reached the end of the road. It was dark. Perhaps J had already come home, turned out the lights, gone to bed? No, the curtains were still open. The flat was empty. It was a big, damp, rented ground floor flat with a rambling 100-foot garden in a converted three-storey house with other tenants upstairs. I could see our sitting room's bay windows, looking out into our road. There were a dozen concrete steps to climb before reaching the communal front door. Outside the window, to my left was a patch of gravelled front garden, with neatly stacked branches and logs cut from the vigorous buddleia tree growing in the North London clay soil. J had pruned the tree back to let in some more light, last weekend, when we had the big row about working too hard and never seeing each other. Taking out his anger with an axe and a hacksaw in the few hours when he was not at the office.

I crossed the road, fumbling for my keys in my handbag, let myself into the communal hall, ignored the pile of post, and opened the front door of our flat, which had a Chinese Pa Kua symbol nailed to it to ward off evil. I kicked off my sandals. My feet hurt, my legs and shoulders ached, my head felt as if it was being gripped by a vice. Without turning on the lights, I walked into the flat and got some painkillers and a glass of water from the kitchen, switched the kettle on. I sat down heavily while I waited for it to boil, my head in my hands.

Then I took some paracetamol, brushed my teeth and washed my face in the kitchen sink, still feeling ill. I made a cup of tea and got into bed. I no longer felt drunk, just shattered. Tomorrow I would probably have a hangover. I needed to stay hydrated. Reaching for the mug in the darkness, I managed to knock the mug onto the bed, spilling hot milky tea all over myself and soaking the duvet. Swearing, I dragged the duvet into the bathroom, and rinsed off the spill, before it stained, and left the wet duvet draped over the bath in the bathroom. I put my huge dressing gown on instead, and wrapped myself up in that, closed my eyes, desperate to get to sleep. I wished J was there. Any moment now, I expected to hear him turn the lock of the front door, undress in the dark and slide into bed beside me, which would probably wake me up again, and tomorrow we would both be irritable with exhaustion. My last conscious thought as I slid into sleep was of resentful anger at J's law firm for doing this to him, and to me, asking him to work so late night after night after night.

I was woken by the chime of the doorbell. I pulled the dressing gown around me and got out of bed, without bothering to switch the light on. I went to the door in the hall, thinking J must have forgotten his key. As I stepped through my door into the communal hall, I could see a figure through the fluted glass panel of the front door, back-lit by the street light outside the house. Although the figure was only a silhouette, I knew it was not J.

I hesitated. The figure was standing close to the glass, trying to see in. Then a voice said, 'It's your neighbour – there's been an accident.'

I could tell by the voice that it was a young man, and the accent sounded West Indian. I knew many of my neighbours. Upstairs was a shy Japanese man who worked in IT, who would bow on the stairs but spoke little English. I knew the older Turkish man with sad eyes who lived next door to the right, whose wife had died, and who now lived alone in a big house, tending the flowers that she had planted in their big garden. We used to talk over the fence when I was outside in our garden, and sometimes swap tomatoes that we had grown. On the left-hand side were a young couple who were landscape gardeners and I used to talk to them too; I regularly admired their climbers, they would compliment J and me on our hanging baskets. Above the gardeners lived a family who I think was Indian, who would nod and smile when we saw each other but whom I didn't know very well. Across the road, directly opposite our flat lived some young West Indian men who had just bought a new car and who would play loud music and laugh and chat with neighbours and passers-by when they were outside cleaning and polishing the vehicle and installing a new souped-up stereo system.

I thought it must be one of them at the door. I thought maybe a pizza delivery kid had been knocked off his bike or something, and I thought I had once mentioned to the men who lived opposite during a conversation that I knew a bit of first aid. So I opened the door, cautiously. Just a crack, just an inch. I wanted to peer past the silhouetted figure of the neighbour calling for help, so I could look out at the street and see the accident, see if there was anything I could do.

The door was wrenched from my hands, and then a stranger threw himself at me, pushing me back into the communal hall, back through the door of our flat into our hall. It was a blitz attack, overwhelming. I staggered backwards, stumbling over my dressing gown, opened my mouth with shock, but no sound came out, only a gasp. *No. No.* 'But you can't' – I said, stupid with surprise – and then he punched me in the face. As hard as he could, and my head snapped back as the pain exploded, my nose poured blood, and the world whirled, the dark hall and the yellow light from the streetlight shining on the ceiling splintered crazily, and then it began.

I was on the floor, on my hands and knees, panting. I knew this was real, and yet I still could not take it in. I had been asleep in my bed, now here I was in the hall. Safe at home but not safe. I was realising slowly, too slowly that I had made a catastrophic mistake. My instincts had failed me; I had opened the door not to a neighbour but to terrible danger. My head seemed to be filled with dark red clouds. I couldn't think properly, calmly. I knew I needed to get a grip, and evaluate the situation. There was nowhere to run to. I tried to concentrate, and to focus on my surroundings, the rough carpet under my hands, the open door into the hall, the light from the street, the pain across my face. The figure made of shadows, the stranger whose face I could not see, was standing before me. He was not out of breath, but his breathing was excited. He stepped back, as careful as if he were taking a penalty shot, and he kicked me in the chest. Then again, in the ribs, then he aimed at my face, and I curled into a ball, trying to protect myself. I could not shout, I couldn't get my breath to scream. I could only whimper 'please, please'. He did not speak to me. He did not seem interested in anything I had to say.

He grabbed a fistful of my long hair, and pulled my head up, away from my covering hands. I tried to look at him, but I could still only see darkness where his face should be. He was faceless. Voiceless. I could see his chest though, his dark skin was shining with sweat. He was tall, over 6 feet, wiry, muscular. As I looked, he seemed to be taking off his clothes. Tearing off his T shirt. Even then, I did not understand why. I thought he must be here to rob me. I thought, he does not have to hurt me, I will be quiet, let him take my bag and my money if that is what he wants. But it wasn't what he wanted, not straight away.

He forced his T shirt over my head as a hood and I gasped. There was a smell of sweat, an acrid spicy body odour; the T shirt was soft cotton in my mouth. I bit down on it. Now I was bagged and gagged and blinded, on my knees, flailing my hands at the empty air. The beating began again. A warm gush of salty blood as my tongue split. My top lip burst like a ripe tomato. The punch on the nose made me want to vomit with pain. My face was a window smashed by a brick. I was breaking into sharp pieces, disintegrating. Choking under the blood-soaked hood, I felt my dressing gown being torn off me. He kicked my thighs apart, and then he was crouched over me, his hand pushing down on my neck. I couldn't breathe. His hand moved upwards, onto my mouth, pressing hard, I could feel through the hood that his fingers were long and slim and strong. I realised moments later that he was raping me, hard, and that he was talking now, but not to me. He muttered an incantation of curses to himself. *'Bitch. Whore. Bitch. Whore.'* Thrust, curse, thrust, curse; pushing hard, forcing himself hard into me, harder and harder, fasterfasterfaster. *I am being fucked by an angry machine.* The fucking was an extension of his pitiless rage. *It is another way to beat me, after smashing my face, my breasts; he wants to smash me inside as well. I can take it.* I willed myself to relax and not tense up, to minimise the damage. I imagined myself liquid, receptive. I imagined me enclosing him, neutralising the rage, softening the blow, softening him. I told myself that I could cope with this. *Nobody ever got fucked to death.* Thinking of this helped to keep me calm. *Rape, what of it? It does not matter. It does not hurt very much. I am keeping him occupied, at least. This is a good strategy. I have stopped the beating, minimised the danger.*

I kept very still, tried not to flinch. I even rocked my hips a little, as if for a lover, while I moved my mind far, far away. I did not feel any pain, not any more. Even when he bit my breasts, and I felt his tongue, his sharp teeth, the wetness of his saliva on me, and I thought for a moment of werewolves, hyenas, feasting on carrion, and I became winter inside, I did not scream. I caught hold of myself instead, and reminded myself that he is just a man. Just a man. *He thinks I am meat to be chewed and spat out. I am not meat,* I think. *I am Rachel. I will not be dead meat. This does not end here.*

I continued to fall away from what was happening. I pulled all that I was deep into myself, disassociating, springing my mind from the trap of my violated body. *I protect myself by shutting down, going to a place inside where I cannot feel him hurting me, where I can never be reached.* In my mind I was sending out a powerful distress signal, calling out for help. *Perhaps someone will sense it, and come to help me. Perhaps this will stop, and I will be rescued, soon.*

But still the thrusts, the threats continued. And I knew then, suddenly, that nobody would come. *I am on my own.* There is him, and there is me, and there is this crunchy beating and this determined raping, and I do not think he will stop, listen to reason. *I am going to have to rescue myself.*

He jerked and shuddered. He stopped moving in me. He pulled out, climbed off. Then he spoke to me for the first time. He said three words, and he said them in a whisper. '*Don't move, bitch.*'

I could hear him moving in the flat, into the bedroom about eight feet away. I shook my head, and I pulled the hood up, enough to see with my eye that was still open. I could hear him opening the wardrobe in the bedroom. I could hear hangers moving on the rail. I shook my head, and the T shirt fell down and hung around my neck. My arms began to move, feebly, nails brushing the carpet, fingertips searching for my mobile phone, for hope, for help. I thought I was being quiet. But he heard me, and he came back. I felt too afraid to look at his face. I kept my head down, cringing. 'I'm sorry – please...'

He was angry. 'I told you not to move. Don't speak. Don't move. *Don't you ever say a word, bitch.*' He swung his leg back again, and kicked me as hard as he could. It knocked the breath out of me. I fell down and curled into a fetal position. *Oh God. He isn't going to stop.* Then I felt him manhandling me and yanking my arms behind my back and tying my wrists, tightly. And fear ran through me like shivering ice-cold water and I started to shake and shake. He was fumbling at his clothes again, pushing my face down into the carpet. *I can't breathe.* I twisted my head to the side, so I could get some air, my hair was too much in my face, it was sticking to the blood, my nose was blocked with blood. *Breathe, breathe, as long as I breathe it will be all right.* He began shoving himself at me, again, trying to rape me again, anally this time, but it did not work, he was too soft. He punched me again, and he bit me, pulling my tender skin in his teeth as I pulled away. The beating began once more. I only wanted it to stop. I knew I would do anything to make it stop. I was his prisoner and I was not sure if I could survive much longer. It came down to each breath in and out, each new blow to absorb, a storm to weather without this boat sinking and going under. It is an effort of will to walk the line between disassociation and unconsciousness. I tried to stay on the right side of it.

Unconsciousness would be a lot easier, I knew, but if I let go, I might not come back.

The blows stopped. He left me on the floor. He went into the bathroom next to the bedroom. This time, I kept still. He returned and crouched down to tie something round my neck. I let him, without protest. I was following my instincts, which told me not to fight, to comply with any demand, any degradation, to stay alive. Then he stood up, and he prodded me with his toe.

'Get up. Get up. Where yo' man now, bitch?' I raised my head, slowly, and shook the T-shirt he had used to hood me away from my head. So I could look at him. I wanted to see him now; I was not afraid any more to see and remember his face because I was not sure that I would be around to describe it to anyone, after this. My looking at him was for me, not anyone else. It was hard to get up, because my hands were tied behind my back, but I managed to roll, so I was kneeling. He used the thing he had tied round my neck to jerk my head towards him, as if I was a dog on a leash. He pulled my head towards his crotch, and I opened my mouth obediently. *Do it, Rachel. Stay alive.* But there was too much blood in my mouth, and as I coughed and choked, a gush of saliva and blood fell out of my mouth and ran down my chin. He seemed to have become disgusted by me, and he jerked away, covering himself.

Now I was deadly afraid, for if he no longer wanted to use me as his plaything, what was left to do with me? We were approaching the last act of this drama. And this time, when the beating started again, I could feel myself losing hope. The blows were harder than before, angrier. I thought of the headlines, '*Rape Victim Found Murdered*'. My parents' grief, my family, my boyfriend, stuck at work at his law firm, trying to finish a deal for a client, coming home and finding me gone forever. This is it, then, this is how it is going to end.

And then it came to me, what my instincts had been telling me to do all along. *I cannot fight this, but I can go along with it. I can make my weakness my survival strategy. He wants me to die. Well then, that is what he will get. The only possible survival strategy is to submit, to try to minimise the force before it becomes lethal. And then to play dead.*

I waited for a blow to the head. *That one was not hard enough, hold on, here it comes, here is his foot smashing into my ear, my jaw. Christ, that was hard, that was enough...* I collapsed, gurgled. And then I held my breath. Playing dead used to be my party trick at school. *Pray God it works now. This is all I have left.*

He said 'shit'. He kicked me again, but not hard, he pushed me with his foot. There was silence, apart from his ragged panting. I could not hear my own tiny breaths. I asked God for this small thing: the minimum of breath to keep my brain alive, my blood moving, my heart beating. It was getting darker, and I was leaving the room now, leaving my body behind. *I am almost free.*

I did not care any more about time passing; time was meaningless now. He was still here beside me in the hall. He was moving about, shifting from foot to foot. Then he went back into the bedroom. I could hear him rummaging again. *It does not matter, I am dead. I am no longer here. He cannot hurt me any more.*

When he came back into the hall he had lit a cigarette. He

crouched down, and I could feel and smell his breath, as I held mine. There was a hiss. His cigarette. He has stubbed it out on my face. The wetness of the blood on my face extinguished it at once, causing minimal burning. *It does not hurt.* I did not move. I continued to pretend to be dead, breathing so slowly and so shallowly that I was hardly breathing at all. I was losing consciousness. The darkness around me was gentleness, silence, peace. I let go. Not quite, but almost. There was still a cobweb thread, an echo of a whisper of something too dear to put away so lightly, that still tied me to my beaten body, and so I hung between worlds, still breathing, but no longer feeling, here but not here. In my ears I heard the sound of an ocean, blood moving. I listened to it, and I fell asleep. I did not dream.

PERHAPS TWO HOURS LATER I started to come round. I had been floating in darkness, looking down at my broken body, thinking: *Shall I come back? It's very peaceful here. It's going to hurt coming back into my body.*

Then I jerked as if I had been electrocuted with a cattle-prod. I was suddenly alive again, back in the room, nerve endings, synapses, muscles on fire with the shock of finding myself in a present that was all disorientating pain. An urgent voice was roaring at me. It was my voice, shouting in my head. *He might still be in the house. He might be about to burn the house down. You have got to escape while you can see he is not in the room! Come on, Rachel, wake up, get up, get up, get up!*

The carpet rushed up to my face and I was back in my body, lying on the floor on my side, curled up in a fetal position, with my arms tied behind me. I tried to move. I could not move very much, my body was too heavy to move. I could feel the carpet on my cheek, my tongue stuck on the roof of my mouth, I could taste my own salty blood. I could move my feet. I could wriggle my shoulders. My weak wriggling gradually became stronger. I began to rock, slowly, turned turtle onto my back, and then found I could use my braced wrists to throw my weight forward onto my knees. I could kneel, and then I could stand. *Now we are getting somewhere.* I shook my matted hair from the eye that could still see, and found I was naked with something hanging round my neck. The light shone onto my white belly. The front door of my ground floor flat was open into the communal hall. The light was coming from the street outside. The front door to the street was closed. *So nobody has found me yet.* But I was back now, I was alive, and I couldn't hear him moving in the flat. If I tried now, I might be able to get help.

I was in the hall. The stairs to the upstairs flats were dark, but I could find my way from memory. I managed to stagger upstairs. Here was my neighbour's door. I could not knock; I had no hands to beat on the door. I tried to shout instead. No sound would come out of my mouth so I threw myself repeatedly against their door. Crashing my shoulder and upper arm, again, and again, but it didn't make a very loud noise. No answer. Still no answer. *This is hopeless. Okay, get out then. It is too dangerous to stay here. But I'm naked. My hands are tied. Too bad. Get out.* Okay. *Come on Rachel. You can do this.*

I blundered downstairs again, almost falling down the stairs. I couldn't balance, my legs were giving way underneath me, it was too dark, and I was almost falling. *Get on with it Rachel, this is no time to fall over and give up. Here is the front door.* To open it, I needed to twist a deadlock knob which was at chest height. How the hell I was going to be able to do this with my hands tied behind my back, I did not know.

I put my back to the front door to the street, and raised myself on tiptoes. The knob was within my fingers, but it would not turn. I tried again, and again, and I found that if I bent from my waist and almost dislocated my shoulder, I could unlock it, twisting the deadlock, slowly, carefully, flexing my wrist and fingers slowly, slowly until the door clicked open. I thanked God for years of yoga and dance classes. In a final blast of adrenaline, I stumbled down the concrete steps, spraining both ankles and tearing ligaments, as a police car screeched to a halt. I threw myself across the bonnet. There had been somebody upstairs, after all, and they had dialled 999.

I suddenly found my voice in an earsplitting roar. The two police officers stared at me in total shock. When I was able to speak words I told them to take the bloody noose off my neck. They said they couldn't because it was evidence. I screamed at them and forced them to cut it off. It turned out to be the lead from my electric toothbrush charger. Around my neck was a bloodstained T shirt that stank of sweat and semen.

The officers' radios crackled while I crouched in the back seat of their police car. The police officers began to talk to me, as one of them untied my hands. What was my name, what had happened? *Rachel. Rape.* I told him to go to the flat, said that the man who attacked me might still be there. I told them I wanted to speak to J. I was shaking so much that I couldn't speak properly, the words came out in grunts and gasps. The officer gave me a notepad and pen to write down J's phone number. I tried to write. Only squiggles came out. I couldn't remember how to write the number down. All I could do was cry out my boyfriend's name, while the police tried to calm me, to cover my nakedness with a blanket. I remember blue flashing light shining on the walls of my neighbours' houses and the warmth of the evening air, and the smell of flowers through the open car window, and the blood and sweat on my thighs making my skin stick painfully to the plastic of the car seat beneath me. I asked for water, but they said what was in my mouth was evidence. I don't remember what I said to them then, but I know that I did not cry.

While a call went out for police officers to search the area for the rapist, an ambulance took me to hospital. I lay covered in a blanket, staring at nothing. I do not remember the journey to North Middlesex hospital. When I got there, I was taken in a wheel-chair to a curtained-off bed in the casualty department. People stared. A police officer stood by the bed, ready, holding his hat. These are only flashes of memory now. Bright lights that hurt my eyes. The sound of the police radio, from behind the curtain. The police doctor carefully noting down all of my injuries on a printed drawing of a woman's body; front, back, side. There were over 40 injuries. Her voice and fingers were gentle as she swabbed my mouth, my private parts, scraped behind fingernails, combed my pubic hair, drew my blood. Said to me in response to my apologies that it didn't matter at all, her being asked to get out of bed and come here, that it was important, that she was sorry to keep me waiting. Then two women police photographers took photographs of the injuries. They were kind, too. I tried to be normal, to be chatty even, to hide my embarrassment at having to thrust my nakedness at the camera. I made bitter jokes about stripping off for naked photos, appearing on a 'battered babes calendar' for a specialist men's magazine. They looked at me with compassion; spoke to me in steady voices. Another nurse stitched my face, and cleaned away some of the blood, though she could not help me with my matted hair. Finally I was allowed a drink of water, to go to the toilet – but one without a mirror. When there were no people scraping and photographing and stitching me and asking me questions, I lay on the bed, looking at the wall. Numb. Waiting. Sometimes I asked for J, and they said he would come as soon as he could, that soon they would bring him to my side.

There was one person who was not kind: a middle-aged doctor who came into the cubicle when I was sitting up. He came over to the bed and gripped my face hard, his hand on my jaw; he turned it from side to side like dog in a show being judged, staring at my stitches but not at me. Still without meeting my gaze, he said to the nurse, 'So, she has been stitched, yes? Then she can go, I think.' His tone of voice made it very clear that me being there, the police, the photographers, everything was a nuisance and that he considered me to blame. I wanted to kill him. I wished I had the strength to slap his hands away and say, '*I am very sorry to inconvenience you by being raped and almost murdered, but do you think you could pay me the courtesy of talking to me like a person rather than a stupid piece of meat?*'

At last J was brought in, and the first words he said were: 'Oh, honey.' He looked into my eyes, as if I was beautiful to him. (Later, he said that my face 'looked like a melted coke bottle'.) He wanted to take my hand, but they made him put on rubber gloves first. That was when I cried, because he was the first person to treat me like a person that night – not as a crime scene or prey – and they wouldn't let him touch me.

The police investigation was as painfully slow as my fight to recover. After five months they arrested an itinerant mugger who had come over illegally from his country, Jamaica, in May 2002. He had beaten and robbed many other women whom he had followed home since his arrival in the UK. His DNA matched that found inside me. He was 17. I had been 31 at the time of the attack.

IN JANUARY 2004 I FACED him in a courtroom. I had changed and he had changed. This time I was stronger and he was weakened. As he lied and blustered I drew my outrage and anger to me like armour and faced him down. When the defence lawyer challenged me, trying to make out that I had propositioned the rapist in the road and invited him in for sex that had 'got out of hand' I felt angry and humiliated but I tried not to let it show. The defence asked to play a video tape of me being interviewed by the police a few days after the attack. In the tape, I said I wasn't sure what had happened, not 100 percent, only 90 percent. The defence lawyer pursed his lips. 'You were not sure then,' he said coolly. 'I put it to you that you cannot be sure now either.' I looked at the judge and I blinked away my tears. I took a deep breath. My voice rang out with more power than I thought that I had ever had before. My gaze was steady. 'I was 90 percent sure then,' I said, clear-eyed. 'I am 100 percent sure now. And I have taken an oath *in front of God* to tell the truth, and I *have* told the truth, about that man there, raping me and beating me. And I stand by it. I am sure. *I know what happened.*' My attacker dropped his eyes first. The defence lawyer said he had no further questions. He sat down. The court was adjourned. The police officer who had led the investigation winked at me and mouthed 'well done'. It was over.

For raping and beating me, and for beating and robbing other women, my attacker was sentenced to 15 years in total. Passing sentence at the Inner London Crown Court, the Judge said:

> *You not only subjected her to a cruel rape, but it was a cruel rape with sadistic violence – much more violence than merely trying to carry out your forceful sex. Not only was it a terrible act and caused great distress, but it continues to cause distress. It is only because of her own bravery in coping with this matter that she is able to lead a more or less normal life. She will never be able to lead a totally normal life because this dreadful incident will remain in her life until the day she dies. You have little insight, you had little idea or feelings as to why you committed these offences and therefore little remorse. Punishment is richly deserved.*

And it was finally over. I had been lucky; fewer than 5 percent of rape cases make it to trial, and the conviction rates are horrifyingly low. I wanted to see if I could do something to help other rape victims come forward. I hoped they could see that it was possible to make your rapist pay, that the police were kind, and diligent, that there could be justice. I waited until most of the worst of the post-traumatic shock symptoms were under control, because I wanted to be sure that I was protecting myself from the consequences of telling my story publicly. But I remembered how I had searched and searched for stories like mine, and how when I had found them, I had read them again and again, and how they had given me hope that, despite what the Judge had said at sentencing about me never having a normal life, I could heal and things would get better. There weren't many stories that told of surviving sudden overwhelming violence from a stranger, and those that I found in newspapers told you only about the attack itself, not much at all about what happened afterwards. There was almost no information on living with the symptoms of post-traumatic shock, the disabling aftermath of overwhelming trauma, or its sometime-follow-up, post-traumatic stress disorder, or PTSD, the strange set of reactions that could appear in survivors months or even years after the mind and body had been overloaded with fear in the face of unexpected extreme danger or the body exposed to the sudden threat of violent death. This made me determined to speak out as soon as I felt strong enough.

It was a year before I felt able to talk to a journalist about what had happened to me. She wrote the story in the first person, in a few hundred words. It wasn't how I have just told it to you now, but it was enough for me to remember it all again, as I read it for the first time. This was the story I was reading – and reliving – on the Piccadilly line three years later in the minutes before I was blown up.

CHAPTER TWO

Aftermath

TODAY I AM A THIRTY-SIX-YEAR-OLD ex-strategy director, who has become a writer. I didn't write before 7th July. Now, I write every day. I have given up my job to dedicate myself to writing. I still live in North London. I am still very much in love with J. I grew up in a Norfolk vicarage with my brother and a sister, loving reading, dancing, art. I studied English and Theology at university, taught English abroad before settling into a career in advertising in London. Before the first attack on me I had few reasons to fear strangers. I was innocent of the overwhelming and implacable hatred that some young men harbour. My life was ordinary, sometimes stressful, usually busy and generally good.

I look back at that time, and it is like looking back through the wrong end of a telescope. That headstrong, determined, passionate, selfish girl seems a long way away. The seventeen-year-old stranger-rapist had yet to unleash his fists on me; nineteen-year-old Germaine Lindsay had yet to detonate his suicide bomb. In photographs my face seems more than just younger; my eyes are different, my top lip is unscarred. It is hard living now with the knowledge that two strangers wanted to hurt me yet did not even know my name. They had never spoken to me. They knew nothing about me. How do you go on living your ordinary life with this knowledge and first-hand experience of violence and evil?

At first after the rape I used my anger to protect me and to fire me up. I fought against sinking into despair; instead I struggled to understand what had happened to me and why. I needed explanations. Why me? I read everything I could, especially other people's accounts of surviving rape. I learned about criminal law, sentencing patterns, psychology, criminal profiling, arguments about nature and nurture, genetics and social conditioning. I read about violence, why men attack women, why people attack people. I would not admit I was afraid, but in truth I was deeply frightened. When I could be attacked in my own flat, where could I feel safe? Whom should I fear? Whom should I trust? Certain sounds, certain smells could cause me to double up, breathless, with a panic attack. In my dreams I fought off faceless monsters made of shadows. Psychologically I was often strangely dissociated and numb. I began to feel incredibly alone. Little I read made me feel any better; understanding brought no comfort, no healing. I began to fear for my sanity.

What brought me back was the gentle, protective love of J, my family and friends. I realised that what I was suffering from had a name, PTSD, post-traumatic stress disorder, that it was a psychological injury that would heal in time, and that I was not going mad.

I started to write about my experiences, anonymously, on an internet discussion board. I was encouraged and supported by strangers. If I still could not make sense of the event, why it had happened, that was because there was no sense, no meaning in it. Wrong place, wrong time, bad luck. The world had always contained danger and it had crossed my path. It was not an attack on me, Rachel; I could have been any woman. I began to realise that when I was attacked I was faceless and dehumanised: I was the Other, Nothing, No One, Not Human. The attacker, by unleashing his hate and his rage against me, was seeking some kind of release. If I started hating and fearing other people – young men, let us say – I risked in some ways becoming like him. I saw how fear and anger makes people isolated and alone, how it breeds despair and more anger, more fear, self-obsession, alienation and eventually corrosive hatred.

He had told me not to speak, but I spoke out. He told me not to tell, but I told. He had wanted me to feel helpless and degraded and frightened, but here I was, telling my story to the police, then to other people, then to a judge. He wanted me to be ashamed, but here I was smiling into other people's faces. The more I listened and talked to other people, the more the numbness thawed. By allowing myself to say I had been afraid, I was winning against the paralysing anger and fear. By making myself vulnerable, I was becoming stronger. It was not easy, but life became richer, sweeter, more vibrant and joyful than before, because I had the gift of knowing that I was loved and cared for. I felt lucky. When I boarded the train on 7th July this year with my story in *Marie Claire*, I was proud that my life was going so well. I had a wonderful new job; my partner and I were celebrating six years of being in love with each other; we had bought our first flat; we had been enjoying a summer of growing flowers and tomatoes in our garden, catching up with friends, dancing, cooking and drinking wine. The *Marie Claire* feature was a story of hope. I wanted to help other women to come forward and seek justice after being assaulted.

A ND THEN THE YOUNG MAN detonated his bomb, seven to ten feet away from me.

I was once more on the floor, in darkness, struggling under a heavy, gasping body. Once more the overwhelming blow to the head, the utter darkness, the blindness, the struggling for breath. Once more the wet on my face. Is it sweat? Is it blood? Is it my blood or someone else's? Do I still have a face? Am I still here or am I dead? But this time I was prepared. By the strange chance of my having just read my own near-death story I was ready. This time it would be different. This time I was not alone.

Immediately after the bombs, people asked me to tell them exactly what it was like. They said they couldn't imagine it. For a while I couldn't find all the words to tell them, to describe the memories that would suddenly rush into my mind and overwhelm me, throwing me back in time. Traumatic shock had numbed me and blanked out the most unbearable details from my memory in the days after the bomb. The broken journey had become a waking dream that haunted me, a puzzle I couldn't solve. The terrifying breathless crash of a past sensory overload felt in the body and unwillingly re-experienced, rather than objectively remembered. An old reality smashing into the present normality, leaving my mind fractured and overwhelmed, and me standing there, unable to explain why I was pale and shaking, mouthing apologies. Day after day, the bomb would explode in my head, over and over, and appalling shards of memory would rain down and pierce my consciousness; trying to place them in order was as futile as trying to put together a shattered mirror.

Despite, or perhaps because of, the prevalence of unwanted 7th July imagery and memories in my life, I was compulsively drawn to any TV programme, any news report that was about 7th July or terrorism. It was a frantic effort to try to understand what had happened, and to control the unmanageable and intrusive re-experiencing of parts of the bomb experience by forcing myself to immerse and focus on the whole story, instead of just my bewildered part in it. One night, I was watching a television documentary about the bombings. I immediately began to have the usual terrifying flashback experiences. But this time, instead of blocking them out by reaching for the whisky, I went straight to my computer, and I typed them out as they hit me, one after another, downloading the remembered horrors, shaping the tastes and textures into sentences, putting them into my internet diary, letting them out of me and giving them to anyone who wanted to read them. It was like gently, painfully cleaning pus out of a seeping wound. I was sorry for the people who were going to read it. But I was becoming frantic; I could not carry this on my own anymore. So when people kept saying, tell me, tell me everything, I did, in the end. This is what it was like in the moments after the bomb exploded.

Night diving, without a regulator. Breathing in liquid, drowning. The taste of blood. Sharp grit in my mouth. Choking, lung-filling dust. It was no longer air that I breathed but tiny shards of glass, and thick, heavy dust and smoke. Like changing a vacuum cleaner bag and pushing your face into the open dust bag and taking deep breaths. It made my tongue swell and crack and dry out like leather. I never covered my mouth. I had nothing to cover it with, and there didn't seem any point. There was a metallic wet taste in my mouth, like vaporising copper particles. It tasted like sucking a coin. That was the blood. It sprayed us, our clothes, our faces, our hair. My lips were wet with it. The walls dripped with it. It was black blood, viscous like oil, because it was mixed with the smoke.

The temperature rose. There was an acrid smell of chemicals and burning rubber and burning hair. It filled my nose. It took over the memory of every smell I remembered and wiped it out. It burned into my mucous membranes. At first my ears were deaf. The explosion had punched my eardrums so violently that my cheekbones and sinuses and teeth rang with it and ached with it. Then I heard the screams. They did not sound human.

I realised that I was on the floor and that there were bodies lying on top of me. The bodies were squirming. *I am alive. They are alive.* My hand locked into another woman's hand. I hissed air out, patted my legs, arms, *they are still here*. I heard a voice, far away. A hubbub of murmurs and an endless scream that did not seem to draw breath, ever. There was a tinkle of glass falling. I squeezed the hand and a voice said, 'Are you all right? Stand up. Stay calm.' It was my own voice. Other voices said the same thing. And I tried to stay hopeful; to stay calm. *I have trained for this. My body and mind know what to do.*

Time passed, slow underwater time, I saw the shapes of bodies in the darkness moving; still the appalling screaming continued. The greeny-yellow emergency lights in the tunnel walls came on, and as the smoke billowed out through the buckled, smashed windows, a little light, a little air began to come into the ruined horror of the carriage. Some more passengers were standing up now; they were appealing for calm, asking for quiet, calling out with me to listen to the injured. Some of us used our mobile phone LED screens for light. People near me took each other's hands, asked each other if they were all right, asked what has happened? *Oh God, save us.* Behind, still, the terrible screams, and now soft groans. Something bad beyond words had happened behind us, but we could not see it, only hear it, and my mind would not try to guess it, not now, not yet. The groans were from people who were very badly injured; I knew this, but I didn't say it, because something told me not to. I looked back into what remained of the first carriage, and I caught a glimpse in the almost-darkness, of bodies on the floor, and of something else, something so horrific that I could not bear to see it. But it was still too dark to see very much, and I did not, could not look again. There were too many people around me to know the full extent of the carnage and destruction; other people's bodies were still protecting me from the worst of the bomb, and its aftermath. It was hard to hear the injured people's fainter cries, because of the loudness of the terrified screaming. The people standing up near me were shouting again; as the temperature rose, it became extremely hard not to panic. It seemed likely that we would die here, trapped underground, burned or choking to death from smoke inhalation – *for surely there is a fire, there is so much smoke now*. Or perhaps we were to be buried alive in a collapsing tunnel. *This is how it is all going to end, then. Here, now, soon.*

There was very little air. It took everything I had not to join in the screams, to stampede. Only the thought that if I was going to die I was not going to die screaming and clawing like a trapped animal held me back. And there was no room to stampede, anyway. I knew then that there was only one hope, and it lay in remaining calm, working together to avoid panic, trying to look after each other. Somehow people around sensed this too, and I heard other voices joining mine, saying to their fellow-passengers near them, 'Hold on, we'll be okay, don't panic, stay calm, it's going to be all right'.

'Keep holding hands. We are going to get out of the tunnel. Stand up, if you can, we need to listen for the injured,' I kept shouting into the darkness. A man near me was calling out the same thing, his voice sounded authoritative and it helped people to calm down. Further up the carriage was another voice imploring everyone not to panic. And behind me, further back in the carriage, still it went on, the terrified screaming of a woman, her screams drowning out what I was straining to listen for, the soft cries of those too weak to scream. The woman next to me began to sob softly. 'I can't see, what's happening, oh God...'

'That woman, she is screaming because she is panicking,' I said. 'It's okay, people who are really hurt don't scream like that. If we stay calm, that will help her calm down.'

I realised then that something was happening at the front of the carriage. The driver was not dead after all. *Shush, listen to his voice.* He was telling us we must leave the train. Underneath my feet as we shuffled forwards, queuing politely to escape the hell scene, was the crunch of broken glass, the rustle of newspapers dropped by passengers as they fell forwards, thrown to the floor by the force of the explosion. And here were hands steadying me down the ladder of the driver's cab, a soft Scottish voice warning us not to step on the live tracks.

The screams were fading as we walked away down the narrow tracks. My ears rang. My eyes swam. I started to pant, because *this is so hard.* And now we were walking in single file through the greenish light of the narrow smoke-misted tunnel and I heard myself saying that *there is hope, there is help, just walk, they are waiting for us all. With water. With blankets. With ambulances and oxygen. Nurses, doctors, helpers, rescuers, all waiting, they will be there, and all we have to do is keep putting one foot in front of the other to get to them, to tell them where the train is trapped.* I said it aloud, again and again, like an incantation, a charm against more disaster, to drown out the groans of the seriously injured man who was being half-carried on another man's shoulders, the two of them braced together, stumbling behind me. The women walking near me listened; they walked; we all walked. We spoke politely to each other. We tried to make jokes. We encouraged each other. We babbled to make a kind of normality, to quell the panic, and our voices drowned out the sobs of pain of the injured man behind. *Can he hear us? Is he dying?* We women walked softly, carefully, looking at our bloodied and blackened feet on the uneven tunnel floor. It took fifteen minutes to walk down the tunnel to Russell Square. *Lights will guide us home.*

As we walked, I was worrying that another train was going to come and crash into us all. I looked for alcoves, places in the wall to press myself against, if it came. I thought about whether I would have time to shout a warning. I imagined us all being mown down – more carnage. I wanted to scream with fear, but I didn't. Instead I said to the woman near me that we were almost there. 'Look, there is a light at the end of the tunnel. It is the long walk to freedom, keep going.' I wanted to believe that we would all be safe and that this would be over soon. The lights in the tunnel were brighter now and I saw something dark and shining poking out of my wrist, jammed into the bone, *oh God, I can see my bone*. It was bleeding everywhere, and I missed my step, staggered, nearly fell, but a woman caught me, holding my arm, telling me not to look at it. A man in a fluorescent jacket appeared, he had come down the tunnel to find us, to tell us the way out, point the way, a messenger of hope, an angel. I reached Russell Square station platform, looked up to see men reaching down. Hands were lifting me off the tracks onto the platform of Russell Square; they pulled on my split wrist; this was the only time I screamed. A small piece of black metal was jerked out of the bone in my wrist and it fell with a 'plink' onto the metal train tracks as I scrambled up, waited a moment crouched on all fours, then stood, and walked slowly, carefully, towards the 'way out' sign.

In the lift, people were falling sideways, eyes staring with shock. In the ticket hall a white-faced man handed out bottles of water. People started to lie on the floor and slump; they were staggering. Some of them were covered in blood. All of them were filthy, with black faces like chimney sweeps. I didn't know what to do to help them. I reached down to a woman who was sitting propped against a pillar, and asked if she was okay. She stared blankly; I could not reach her. She had blood coming out of her ears. I took her hand. It was shaking as if she has been electrocuted. She did not want to look at me. She looked past me with a thousand-yard stare.

I can't see any ambulances outside. We need ambulances. Where are the ambulances? Where are the police? Who is coming to help these people?

I felt trapped and helpless. I thought. *I can't do any more, I have kept calm, I have helped people to escape, I have told them that there will be help when they get here and it isn't my fault that everything is chaos.* The world had shrunk now to my own selfish need to wipe the taste of evil from my mouth. I did not think I could cope with any more of this. I needed a cigarette. *Not in the ticket hall, it's not allowed.* I staggered out onto the pavement, opposite Tesco, by the zebra crossing, snapping open my mobile phone. It was still working.

I did not think to call an ambulance; I assumed they already were on their way. I managed to call J and leave a message on his work voicemail. I was terrified that he was travelling on the train behind me and that he was dead. I said that the train had derailed. My voice was strangely flat, and thickened with a lisp, because my tongue was so dusty and dry. Then I sent him a text as well. I texted that there had been a train accident but I was okay. I knew it was not a train accident, but I did not want to say that I thought it was a bomb. I did not want to believe the evidence of my senses.

I could not light the cigarette; my hand was wet with blood. I realised that I was covered in a sticky black film of chemicals and blood. I knew that not all of the blood was mine. I needed to call work, but I couldn't remember my number, or the name of my company. I couldn't remember the number for directory inquiries. I was in deep shock, like everybody else who had climbed out of the suicide-bombed carriage, but at that moment I did not realise it. I was only in the present, the terrible unreality of this strange present. I needed daylight; I needed to get away from this station, this nightmare. I wanted to run, and run, and run.

I was experiencing one of the three classic reactions to extreme threat: the desire to flee. This was a change from the last time. When I was raped, I froze, and that ability to stay still and to disassociate, that instinct that told me not to fight back and escalate the violence saved my life. This time, when the attack came, I was already in battle mode, heart pumping, body chemistry wired to defend myself against the indefensible, because I had just re-lived the earlier attack. When the bomb exploded, I did not freeze, and I did not fight to escape, and I could not flee, for there was nowhere to run to. Instead I became peculiarly calm, and I helped people to stand up, and begged them to stay calm too, and we kept each other safe from panic, and we waited in line to leave the train, and we walked, carefully down the tunnel and I made jokes to stop the slide into panic and despair. I became a wisecracking embattled soldier in a war zone, focused on surviving the present, helping to keep the team together, keeping up morale, holding the fear at bay to survive. But now we had escaped, my new-found leadership abilities were deserting me and the animal desire to run to safety was kicking back in.

I compromised, and instead of doing what I wanted to do, which was to sprint away from the tube station and hide somewhere, I put my unlit cigarette in my mouth, and I started to look up and down the road for ambulances, and police, and people who could help us.

Standing outside the ticket hall of Russell Square station, I began to calm down. I reconnected with the daylight world outside, realised that I was out of the tunnel. A Japanese tourist was filming me. People were milling about outside, looking irritated. A commuter shouted: 'I need to get to work!' She saw me, came up to me. 'What the hell is going on? I need to get the tube to work!' I was black-faced, shuddering, Einstein-haired. I told her that she wouldn't get to work on the tube today. She mouthed a curse at me. Someone lit my cigarette for me and I took an enormous drag. *Anything to take the taste of smoke and blood from my mouth.*

I found a number on my mobile: a colleague, Jenna. Jenna, in her early twenties, green-eyed, slim, long-legged, gentle and helpful, who worked opposite me. She had passed her first aid course last week. We worked about a quarter of a mile away in the West End. I told her to please come in a taxi; I needed to get to A & E. I said that I didn't need an ambulance. The people I left behind needed the ambulance. I didn't want to think about who I left behind.

A lady came up to me, with pity in her eyes. She offered me a paper tissue for my wrist, and she patted me gently, calling me, 'my dear'. I didn't want to put the tissue on my wrist, because I thought it would dissolve in all the blood, and leave bits and there was already glass and dirt and God knows what in the wound. I held my arm out stiffly, and then I put it on my head, which is what I had done when I was walking down the tunnel. Trying to stop the bleeding. Then another woman came up to me and asked what had happened. A Kiwi, she told me that her name was Anna, she was a nurse, and that I was in shock. I told her no. *It's all right, I am fine.* Then I realised that this was the help that I had been hoping for. I clutched at Anna, and I told her to call an ambulance, and if she is a nurse, please, to go into the station. 'There are people there who are hurt. There are people still stuck on the train, they are screaming, they are hurt, it is stuck in a tunnel.' I was babbling, wide-eyed, telling Anna to please, go, go. Anna looked at me, then she went to the station entrance, where they had pulled the metal grille closed now to stop the bombed people getting out, to stop normal people getting in. I heard her saying that she was a nurse. The grille opened for her and she went to help the people inside.

I started to faint. The supermarket across the road, the people near me started to blur. I leaned on a rail, feeling sick. Then I saw a black cab. The taxi had come, with my colleague Jenna inside; she was waving her green first aid box at me. Jenna looked shocked as she held open the cab door. I realised how I smelled, as the stink of the train and the tunnel and the explosion filled the taxi. Jenna asked what had happened, I told her that there had been an accident on my train to work and that 'people are hurt. They are inside the station and in the train.' I told Jenna to ask if anyone wanted a lift to A&E. Jenna jumped out, and went up to the people outside the station, but they could not hear her. They were deaf from the explosion, or they did not understand, or they were on the other side of the grille in the ticket hall and they could not get out.

The taxi driver looked cross at having to wait with the door open on a zebra crossing. Jenna gave up and got back into the taxi with me. My mouth was numb; my ears humming; I could not see properly. I was panting again. Jenna wrapped a bandage very carefully around my wrist. The taxi drove past Tavistock Square. It was nearly 9.45am. As we left the Square there was a dull 'crump' that made the taxi windows rattle. Later I found out that it was the bus exploding on the other side of the trees.

We arrived at University College Hospital. The taxi driver demanded a tenner for the journey. I passed it over. I switched off. I was focusing now on getting into the casualty department, and telling the hospital that they needed to send ambulances to Russell Square. I was still feeling strangely numb, but also anxious, because I knew that I shouldn't be here, walking towards the hospital foyer, with Jenna at my side. What I felt was guilt. *She shouldn't be here, I shouldn't be here, and people at this hospital should not be wasting their time faffing about with me, not when I know that there are so many more people who are injured, who are much worse. I should be at my desk at work. Everything was terribly, terribly wrong. All of those people are still back at Russell Square, and I am here, and I couldn't, didn't help them.*

A man in a yellow fluorescent jacket was standing in the hospital foyer, as I strode through the doors. He held up his hand to check me. I barely slowed down, Jenna hurrying just behind me. 'My train exploded,' I said, 'and I need to tell people what happened.' He looked shocked. Waved me through, to the A & E desk, where I gave my name, and was given a wristband, which told me that there had been a major incident and that I was casualty number eleven. It was becoming clear that the hospital was already geared up for a major incident, and everyone was following a practised protocol. Now I could see the doctors and nurses, who had started to gather, ready for the injured that they knew were coming, and I started to tell them, as best I could, as they picked the glass out of my arm, as they cleaned it, as they X-rayed it, what I knew about what had happened to the hundreds of people on the westbound Piccadilly line rush-hour train.

CHAPTER THREE

Hospital

A SHORT WHILE LATER, AS I sat on a bed looking at my new stitches, apologising to the nurse for making the sheets so filthy, another nurse popped in and pointed out that I was 'completely black in the face'. She told me to wash, so I made a mess in a small sink, splashing black water all over the floor. My hands were still shaking. My nails were black, not just under my nails, but the cuticles, the creases on the skin in my hands. The soap stung my face, and my hair was like straw, my tidy brunette ponytail now a fright of grey tangles. I found some moisturiser in my bag, and I rubbed it into my face and hands. I now had a greasy, grey face instead of a caked, black one. Every time I moved, small pieces of glass fell off me and dropped to the floor. My ear was itching; I found a piece of glass in it. Then another, and another. There was glass in my bra, in my shoes, everywhere. My head was pounding, and I remembered that I had some codeine tablets in my handbag. I took two.

Jenna was sitting on a chair, showing the nurse her first aid kit, and answering questions about what had happened. She was telling the nurse what I had told her, that there had been a train accident. I began to accept that it was a bomb, and that I had known this almost as soon as I got up off the floor of the carriage and smelled the smoke and explosives. I remembered that I had been keeping this information to myself, because I didn't want to cause a panic on the train or at the station. It occurred to me that there was no need to censor the information any more, and so I told the nurse that there had been a bomb. She looked hard at me. 'Really?' she said, still staring. Then she went away. I wanted to call out after her. *Yes, really. There really has been a bomb on my train. I know it doesn't make sense. But that's what happened.*

It started to hit me then; that the screaming, which I had told fellow-passengers next to me was just people panicking, was not just screaming because we were stuck in the dark and it was a scary situation. It was the screams of people who thought they were about to die. The groans that I had heard were the groans of people who were very seriously injured, possibly dying. I knew why I had said what I said about the screams to the other passengers when we were trapped; it was to prevent a panic. Because what could we do? We had to get off the train, and tell people what had happened, so help could get to the stricken train. There were too many of us, it was too dark, too crowded, too full of smoke, too full of glass and bent metal. There were no first aid kits on board. We would have trampled the people who were badly hurt in the dark. I started to get angry with myself, because I thought I had somehow failed the injured passengers, and that I had done the wrong thing in leaving the train. Then I thought: but we were trapped. We were told to get out. What were we supposed to do? I told these things to the man who was stitching my wrist. My voice was too calm, too measured, as I asked his opinion on the correct procedure for evacuating an exploded train. He let me talk as he worked; then he told me that I had done the right thing. 'You were a casualty,' he said, 'and you needed to come here and get stitched up. That is what we are here for.'

I was still distressed. 'But what about all those other people on the train who were badly hurt? I don't really need to be here, people should be looking after them, not me.'

He pointed out again that I was a victim myself, and that I was still in shock, because I had been hurt as well. Then he said that my stitches looked fine and as I had stopped bleeding, why didn't I go and have a cup of tea? He looked at Jenna, and she came over, and took my arm. As we left, a man was brought in on a trolley. He was sobbing, and whimpering quietly, and he was covered in blood. His leg looked like raw meat. The other leg was not there. Jenna went tense; I told her not to look, 'Come on, let's go.' A young woman came up to me and introduced herself as an intern, and she led us away back to the hospital foyer, and then to a lounge, where she said we could have that cup of tea.

The lounge had lots of plastic chairs, with about ten people sitting down, a tea/coffee machine, and no windows. The area was being managed by a volunteer, Faith, a nurse who had come in on her day off to help out. She took my name, and Jenna's name, and showed us where we could sit down. I texted J to say that I was in hospital and I'd had stitches and was ok and with a friend so no need to leave work. I tried to make the message as normal as possible, because I didn't want to think of J caught up in all of this too. I wanted to imagine him safe at his desk, working on a deal for his client, looking at documents, drinking coffee, not being worried.

A teenage girl in a short party dress limped past. She had her leg in plaster below the knee, and she was cross that she could not get through to anyone on her mobile phone. She complained repeatedly that she was going on holiday this afternoon, and what would she do with her foot like this? She would not be able to swim or sunbathe on the beach. It was a nightmare, she repeated, an absolute nightmare, she could not possibly think of a worse thing to have happened.

A middle-aged lady with short hair and a kind face sat quietly near me, and I asked her what she was in for. She said that she'd had a heart attack last night, and had spent the night in a bed at the hospital. Then, she was asked to get out of her bed this morning and come and wait down here, because the hospital needed all the beds for a major incident with multiple casualties.

I was shocked by this; if they were turfing people with heart attacks out of their beds, then I knew that we were in big trouble. She asked me if I knew what had happened, what the major incident was? I told her that I didn't know if it was the same thing, but there was a bomb on the Underground train. She put her hand to her mouth. She asked me if I was on the train. 'Yes,' I said, 'I was on the train.' 'Is that why your face is so dirty?' she asked. 'Oh my God, you poor thing.' She wanted to ask more questions, but she didn't want to upset me. She turned to Jenna, whose face was clean, and asked her if she was involved. Jenna said no, she just came with me to hospital. She showed the lady her first aid box. The lady said that was handy, that she happened to be carrying that on her. Jenna started to explain that she didn't normally walk about with a first aid kit; that she was at work; that she was the office first aider, and so she had come and got me in a taxi when I called her.

This struck me as being very funny, the thought of Jenna walking about with her big green first aid box at all times, after she proudly qualified as a first aider last week, and I started to laugh and laugh. A nurse came over and offered me a tissue, because she thought I was sobbing. Then she saw that I was having a fit of the giggles. She told me that I must have a cup of tea. With sugar. I started to protest that I didn't have sugar, and she said, firmly, that today I did because I was in shock. She told Jenna to keep an eye on me. I stopped giggling. I shut up and drank the tea: it was dishwater grey in a plastic cup, teeth-grittingly sweet and absolutely horrible.

Somebody turned on a small television in the corner. The BBC news was on. There was a news ticker running across the screen and I saw that it said that there had been power surges on the London Underground and the whole system was shut down. There was a picture of a bus with the roof torn off on the screen. The presenters were explaining that there had been an explosion on the bus. This did not make sense. The explosion was on the train. I did not understand what the news could mean about the power failures. I could not understand what was going on.

The teenage girl with her leg in plaster had noticed the news too. She asked me what had happened. 'I don't know,' I told her. I tried to listen to the television. The girl stood beside me, watched the news, as the presenters announced that there were no trains running, that the Underground was closed.

'I wonder whether the trains to the airport are running. What a total nightmare. I need to go on holiday. How am I going to go on holiday? What am I going to do?' she asked.

'I really don't know,' I said. I wished she would shut up.

Everybody in the room was now watching the news, and the picture of the exploded bus on the screen. The presenters were still saying that there had been power surges on the Underground. That there had been a major incident. They read out a list of stations; one of them, King's Cross. They said that there were reports of injuries and 'walking wounded'. It started to dawn on me that they were still saying that what had happened on my train was a power surge, but I knew that this was wrong. *It was a bomb. Like the bomb on the bus. What is the matter with them?*

Power surges don't blow out windows and rip off doors. They don't tear people's legs off. And if they are saying power surge and I know it was a bomb, then there must be more than one bomb. London is under attack.

As I stood by the television thinking this, somebody came into the room and announced that nobody could leave because we were under attack. At least, I think this is what they said, because they were immediately shushed. There was a hasty conference of nurses in a corner. I looked at Jenna, she looked puzzled and anxious. All of us could do nothing apart from keep watching the news. I still hadn't heard from J. I could not get through on the phone to him, or to my parents. I sent a text asking them to get in touch. Then I texted my sister and my friend Jane as well.

HAVE ESCAPED FROM BOMBED TRAIN WALKED DOWN TRACK. AM IN HOSPITAL HAD STITCHES ALL OK PLEASE CALL & SAY U R OK.

I was desperate to get away from here now, and to find J. I texted him again to say that they were keeping us in hospital but as soon as I could escape, please come and get me. The phone beeped back. It was a message from J. He was alive! He was in the office. He told me to stay there, to look after myself, that he loved me. I was indescribably relieved that he was all right. Now all I wanted to do was to see his face.

I asked Faith, who was doing a sterling job in charge of the lounge, if I could go yet. She said no. I said that I really wanted to have a cigarette and she agreed that I could go outside and have one. Somebody would come with me. Jenna offered, but the nice intern who had led me to the lounge came over and said she would take me, because I needed to go and see the police as well. I apologised to Jenna for wasting her morning like this. She said she didn't mind. She would stay here and watch the news and tell me if anything came up.

I went outside, where it was starting to rain. I felt very weird, still numb, and still slightly dizzy. *It must be the codeine tablets*. Three more text messages came through, from my parents and my sister and from my friend Jane. Thank God, now they knew I was safe and I knew that they were okay. I sat on the steps, feeling relief, and looked out at Euston Road, which seemed very quiet. Perhaps they were not letting traffic through. I breathed smoke out of my mouth, slowly, and watched it drift into the grey rainy air. The intern had gone back inside. The rain fell on me, I turned my head to the sky and opened my mouth, tasting the rain on my lips, and closed my eyes. I became aware of someone near me, looking at me, and opened them again.

'Can I talk to you? I'm from the *Financial Times*.'

How odd, I thought. I don't know anything about economics.

'Can you tell me what happened?'

He didn't ask if I was there. I realised he probably didn't have to, looking at me.

I told him what had happened. I did not mention my belief that it was a bomb. I simply described the 'almighty bang', how everything went black, how I feared I had gone blind, the crying and struggling, how we kept each other calm and even made jokes, saying if anybody's boss gave them grief 'we are going to tell them where to get off'.

He described me in the article the next day as 'still shaking with shock, her face grey, her fingernails blackened from the dust hurled up by the blast, a deep gash to her right arm'. He thanked me for the interview, and we talked briefly about the latest news before he walked away.

Then I saw a woman with a blackened face nearby, she was cringing as another reporter and a camera man held a microphone into her face and she was stammering 'I don't know' to the journalist's repeated questions. I exchanged a look with her, she looked shocked and desperate, and I called out to the reporter, who looked uncomfortable, 'Do you want to talk to me instead? I've got time. I'm having another cigarette.'

He came over, and she mouthed 'thank you' to me, and she darted into the hospital, where security guards were not letting the media through. I talked to that reporter as well. Then I went back inside.

I could see that there were multiple casualties who had made their way here now, or perhaps they had been brought in ambulances; the hospital was extremely busy, but there was a controlled, organised sense of purposefulness. I wandered back into the A&E reception area by mistake, because I was disoriented and I could not remember where the lounge was. I saw a woman who could not remember her name, anything, being questioned gently by someone from the hospital. I felt again this odd sense of deep shame that I was there. All I wanted was to quickly get stitched up and to go, if not to work, then at least to somewhere normal, like a café or a pub. I really wanted a drink.

I was starting to worry about the fact that I had gone completely deaf in one ear and semi-deaf in the other. And my arm seemed to have swollen up a lot too; it was pale pink and puffy with lots of little lacerations in it that looked like black pen marks. My forearm was beginning to ache and feel painful. Some of the lacerations were bleeding again. I asked the reception desk lady if I should get it checked again. She said, yes, probably. But then I thought of how long this would take, how busy the hospital was and of how I could always see a doctor later. I sidled away from her, sideways, like a crab, while promising to get to the back of the queue to get it looked at. The nice intern found me dithering in the foyer, and came over and said that the police wanted to talk to me now. I worried aloud about Jenna stuck in the windowless lounge, but the intern said that she was fine, and it wouldn't take long. I went up some stairs and there were some plainclothes police men and women who introduced themselves as CID officers. They said that they needed to find out as much as possible about what happened. I gave them my details. They filled in a form. When they got to the part about my physical build, the officer smiled at me and said 'I'll put slim/medium'. I thanked him for being a gent.

Then I went through the whole story again. I told them that I was sure it was a bomb, not a power surge. They asked me why I thought that. I explained about the smell of explosives and the bang and the devastation. I told them where I was on the train, how I was in the front carriage, how we escaped through the driver's cab and how we evacuated to Russell Square. 'Not King's Cross?' they asked.

'No, Russell Square, it took ages to walk down the tunnel, we had only just left King's Cross.' They looked at each other. They asked if I had seen any damage to the tunnel, when I got off the train. I thought hard, and said no. 'That means the bomb must have been behind me', I told them. 'Maybe further back in the train. I'm not sure where. I'm still alive, so it can't have been near me.'

I asked them how many people were dead. They said that they didn't know yet. The news was still talking about 'casualties' and 'walking wounded'. But I knew it was worse than that. There was a man who was brought in with one of his legs ripped off, for a start. I saw things before I left that carriage... I did not want to tell them what I thought I saw. If I didn't say it out loud, I could tell myself that it was not real. I asked them again. How bad was it? They told me that they didn't know enough at the moment to say. They said that it looked as if I had been very lucky.

They asked if they could take my photograph. I asked if they wanted me to smile. They looked at me as if I was a bit strange. I sat on a chair in a room and held up my bandaged arm, as requested. The photographer said that I didn't look my best, but not to worry about it for today. I said at least I had washed my face, and he said in surprise, 'Have you?'

A woman police officer informed me that she needed to take my clothes and bag for forensic purposes. 'We'll give you a nice tracksuit instead.'

I baulked at this. I negotiated with them, I said that I was sure now that I was not very near the bomb, and please, please, can I keep my clothes? 'This is my new expensive suit, my new top, my favourite shoes, my new bag...' It was too much like being in hospital after the rape, having no clothes, being depersonalised, though I didn't say that. I practically begged them to let me keep my clothes on. In the end they gave me some brown paper bags and asked me to put the clothes and bag and shoes into the bags and then to seal them when I got home, and they said they would call me if they needed them. And then they wished me good luck, and they let me go, and I went back downstairs again with the intern, and she took me back to the lounge.

I asked the nurses if I could leave. I just wanted to get out of there. Faith came over and explained that they needed to keep everyone here for at least four hours, so that they could be monitored for shock, and breathing difficulties and internal injuries. I told her that I was positive that I didn't have breathing difficulties; I had smoked at least four fags since I'd got off the train and I was fine. I said that I would be with someone who could watch me for shock. She said that I could go if a doctor gave me the all-clear. She asked one of the nurses to see if she could find a doctor to check on me. I looked at my wrist. My hand and arm and fingers were very swollen, and the little glass lacerations now looked like bad tattoos, oozing black inky droplets but the deep gash had definitely stopped bleeding. Apart from the fact that I stank, and was filthy, and that I felt very wired on adrenaline, and a bit floaty and disorientated, I felt okay. I desperately wanted to see J. They had turned off the news now. Probably to stop everyone getting in a state.

Jenna was being brilliant. She said that she didn't know what to do really, but she was happy to stay with me as long as I needed her to. I explained that I was mad keen to get out of there and she said that sounded like a good plan. We sat together, holding hands, hoping to get out soon. After about twenty minutes a junior doctor came in and asked me some questions, and instructed me to go to my GP at once if I felt sick or had a headache or felt faint, and to make sure that I had someone with me all the time, and then said I could go. I texted J.

THEY ARE LETTING US OUT. PLEASE COME AND GET ME. WILL TEXT WHERE I AM. COME TO UCH.

OUTSIDE THE HOSPITAL IT WAS grey and rainy. Euston Road was completely deserted. We could walk right across the normally busy dual carriageway, to a café across the road opposite the hospital called SNACKSTOP. Inside, I sat down and we got some cups of strong tea. Without sugar this time. Neither Jenna nor I knew what to say to each other. I kept thanking her, she kept saying that it was nothing, and she was no use, and I kept telling her that she was brilliant. And wasn't it funny that she had qualified as a first aider only last week; nobody would ever have guessed that she would be using her skills in a major terrorist attack a few days later?

I realised what I had just said. Major terrorist attack. The enormity of all this was too huge to take in. One minute I was reliving being raped and tortured and almost killed, while standing up on a train going to work, then it went black and I was lying on the floor and someone was screaming that we were all going to die, then I was walking down a tube tunnel, then I was in hospital, then I was being photographed by the police, and now I was sitting in a café with a girl from work whom I had known for six weeks and we were discussing being caught up in a major terrorist attack together. No wonder it was hard to have a normal conversation. I drank my tea quietly and texted unnecessarily complicated directions to J about where the café was. He texted back to say he was walking over from his office in the City. Jenna asked me if I wanted a sandwich. I didn't, even though it was now past midday and I had eaten nothing all day. It rained harder outside the café. Then the rain abruptly stopped and the sun came out.

A woman who was sitting at the table behind me leaned over and said she was sorry to interrupt us but she was a reporter and could she please get my story. Okay. I told the story again. Already it was starting to feel like it had happened to somebody else. She asked me for my mobile number. I gave it to her.

I said sorry again to Jenna for getting her dragged into all this and explained that J was on his way, she must be fed up, and did she want to go home? Jenna said that she was not leaving until J arrived. I asked her how she was going to get home to South London, as it was obvious that nobody could use public transport, not after what had happened. Jenna said that she had her trainers, and that she would run home.

I was filled with admiration, and with gratitude to her, for her calmness, sweetness and common sense. I felt a bit weepy at the thought of Jenna running home across London in the rain, with her first aid kit in her rucksack. 'I hope that you don't need to do any more first aid today,' I told her.

My phone rang, it was J, he was nearby but he couldn't find the café. We went outside to look for him, and then I saw him, loping calmly across the road, in his suit, with the sun shining on his glasses, coming to find me, smiling at me. I threw myself into his arms, and we had a huge snog that went on and on and on. We broke apart to find Jenna looking smiley, but slightly embarrassed. I started to babble about how great she had been, and J thanked her, and they shook hands, and she hugged me. And then Jenna said she thought she'd scoot off and leave us to it, and off she ran, down the deserted Euston Road, running home across the wet, grey city where nothing was normal anymore.

J and I looked at each other. 'Pint?' he said. 'Pint,' I agreed. Seeing his face was wonderful. I started to shake with the relief of being alive.

CHAPTER FOUR

Getting home

B Y THE TIME WE GOT to the pub, which was ten minutes away, J and I had updated each other on the morning's events. He told me of a helicopter hovering over his office near Ludgate Hill, the realisation of what had been going on as the news of the bombs began to break, the slow sickening understanding that I had not been in a train derailment at all but caught up in a terrorist attack. How he wanted to hurry to my side, but was told to stay at his desk, and not leave the building: that his office, near the Old Bailey, was a possible terrorist target. Then how he got my text that I could get out of the hospital and was waiting for him. He had emailed his boss and set out at once. 'I can always trust you to end up in trouble,' he told me, squeezing my hand and holding it tight. I couldn't stop smiling; such euphoria was rising in me that I felt that I could float away from the pavement if it were not for

J's hand anchoring me. I was starting to feel invincible, bomb-proof, elated, as if I had just run a marathon or triumphed in a battle. J could tell that I was extraordinarily high on life, and he went to the bar and got me a cold Guinness and a very large whisky with ice. I drank them while trying to hide behind a pillar, conscious of my strange scarecrow appearance. The alcohol cooled my parched sore throat, but it seemed to make absolutely no difference to how I felt. I had the feeling that I could drink the bar dry and never get drunk, that my body chemicals and I were unassailable today. The pub was full of people drinking and smoking as fast as they could; it was only just after twelve, but there was a noisy hubbub and it was packed. Big screens usually used for watching the football were all showing the news, and everywhere there were pictures of the red double-decker bus, with its roof torn off. The shots of the bus were oddly free of bodies, though the news sometimes showed a shot of blood splashed on the walls of a building.

'They must be holding back on the really terrible images,' I said. (Later, I heard from a picture editor that this was the case.) The bus exploded in Tavistock Square, very near Russell Square, about an hour after the explosion on my train. It was clear that there had been multiple explosions; it was not clear how many bombs had gone off, and the news was now showing dozens of sooty, shocked people coming out of other tube stations, police and ambulances in attendance and seriously injured people being carried on stretchers. I did not understand how it was possible to feel elated and horrified simultaneously.

People were staring at me now in the pub, because I looked

like the people on the news. Except peculiarly cheerful and with a pint in my hand. I suggested to J that we found another pub. We started to walk towards Camden. The streets were full of people walking, some sauntering and chatting to each other, most of them pounding the pavements, grim-faced. It was a great London exodus, as hundreds of thousands of people began what was referred to by all the papers the next day as The Long Walk Home. Among them were numerous survivors who had staggered off three trains and a bus left smoking and devastated. Over a thousand people directly affected by the bombs simply walked away on 7th July, dazed with shock. Many of them were never contacted by the authorities, for nobody took their details and even now, some are still not on an official list. Some of them would contact me, weeks, months later, having read my internet diary, and they would tell me their stories and ask if I could help them to meet others like them. But all that was to come, and for now J and I were simply two of the hundreds of thousands of Londoners putting one foot in front of the other until we found our way home.

My feet, bare in my sandals, were covered in grime and dried blood, and now they were bleeding again, because there was glass caught in the straps of my shoes, but I didn't notice any pain. We walked and walked, and as we walked we called a friend, Jane, who said she would try and pick us up in her car. 'But it's a nightmare, Rach, they're telling everyone London is closed.'

'London "closed"? How can a whole city be "closed"?'

We found another pub about a mile further down the road, with noisy music playing, and a bunch of Australian twenty-somethings chatting excitedly. Everyone seemed to be very drunk, and getting drunker. The Aussies realised immediately that I was One of the Scary Bombed People, but their cheerfulness and friendly concern made me much less self-conscious than before. I began a comedy turn and regaled them with the crap jokes I'd made in the tunnel. 'If anyone's boss gives them any grief for being late, we're going to tell them where to get off, eh girls?' 'C'mon, let's go and get a refund from London Underground!' They cheered, and slapped me on the back. 'Good on you, mate! That's the spirit!' They offered to buy rounds and bags of crisps. Everyone was getting more and more lively and rowdy. It was a great atmosphere.

A dishevelled middle-aged man came over to our group and started shouting and bellowing. He was almost incoherent. He took an empty pint glass and he smashed it on the floor. The jolly atmosphere of bonhomie ceased at once, people froze and became quiet. He was grimacing, spittle-flecked, crimson-faced with rage, his eyes bulging and teary.

'Bastards, bastards... I'm going to kill them, fuck them, fuck them all, *bastards*...'

One of the bar staff came over. 'Mate. Calm down.'

This only enraged him more. He turned, swivel-eyed, and clenched his fists, looking like he was about to take a swing at someone.

Without thinking about whether it was a good idea or not, I leaned over, touched his hand, gently. 'Do you think, sorry, would you mind, not being so loud, only I've got a headache, and I'm still in shock, there was a bomb on my train, I'm a bit freaked out, a bit shaken up still...'

He missed a beat, then his shoulders slumped and he burst into tears. 'I'm sorry, I'm so sorry,' he said, and he started to clutch my hand, pumping it with a huge moist and reddened paw. 'I'm shaken up too. Bastards, *why*? The fucking, fucking bastards...'

The Aussies helpfully pointed at a chair nearby. 'Chill out mate. Have a seat. Have a drink. Have some crisps.' The angry man sat down heavily, quiet now, then he shambled off to the toilets a few moments later. J and I exchanged glances. 'I'll get a round in,' I said.

Later, I found out from an ambulance dispatcher blog that the numbers of calls from 'people going off on one' jumped in the late afternoon and evening of 7th July. I could understand why. Shock, fear and alcohol are a heady combination. Emotions running as high and as fast as a spring river can easily burst their banks. I was cushioned by shock, but I could sense his almost-panic that had turned to incoherent near-hysteria after several pints. It wasn't so far from where I was myself. I called Jane. She said she was on her way, she was nearly there. I was glad. I longed for a shower, a cup of tea, and for a chance to sit down on my own sofa, and to get my head round what the bloody hell had happened to London.

As soon as we got in Jane's car, I was desperate for the loo. I hadn't been to the toilet since 7am, and it was now almost 5pm. I didn't take in much of the journey home, only that the traffic was terrible, and that it took ages, and by the time we got back to our flat I was doubled over in cross-legged desperation. Once I had been to the bathroom, I flumped on the sofa and began mainlining the news of 7th July, flicking from channel to channel, as greedy as a junkie with a stash of what they crave.

I was searching for the story of someone like me, the story of the other people from the exploding Piccadilly line train. I wanted to know who, how, where, what they were feeling. The TV gave me no answers. This bothered me. For now the personal was the political, and the news story was my story. I wanted somebody to tell the story of the darkness of the Underground train. What had happened to me, what had happened to us. Until I heard it from someone else, it was hard to believe that it was real.

It was getting late, J had to work tomorrow. I had a shower. The water ran black for five minutes. Afterwards, I had a bath as well, with rose oil. We went to bed. I couldn't sleep, though J was breathing peacefully now, and the cat was snoring by the bedside as well. My heart was still beating as if I had drunk a pint of strong coffee. I got out of bed, put on a dressing gown. I went to the computer in the other room. There was still a smell of smoke and blood in my nose, in my throat. I was haunted by other people's ghosts, people who were strangers to me, and by the great, pressing weight of a story that would not let me be. I sat down on my chair in the study and I turned on the computer. A few more tiny shards of glass fall out of my hair onto the keyboard. This was a story which seemed to tell itself as my fingers moved across the keyboards. I posted it on the urban75 website, a popular internet bulletin board where thousands of Londoners were swapping news and telling their accounts of what had happened today. I told it anonymously, grateful to be here to tell it. Just one of the many voices from the darkness of the Underground train. I typed:

10.59pm 7th July
I was on a crowded train to work – it was 8.40am

when I boarded the crammed Piccadilly line train at Finsbury Park.

Normally I board half way up the train, but the train was so full, I walked up to the front of the train to board. I was on the first carriage, the one behind the driver's carriage, by the doors; it was absolutely packed, and even more people got on at King's X making it what felt like the most crowded train ever.

Then as we left King's X, about 5 to 9, there was an almighty bang and everything went totally black.

Then clouds of choking smoke filled the tube carriage and I thought I had been blinded. It was so dark that nobody could see anything. I thought I was about to die, or was dead, then I realised I was choking, the smoke was like being underwater, but gradually I could see, a little, as the emergency lights in the tunnel kicked in. The glass was smashed so air started to flood in, we were ok.

There was silence for 10 seconds. Then a terrible screaming.

We all tried not to panic, we said to each other 'ok, stay cool, stand up if you aren't injured, hold hands, don't cry, stand up, hold on, we'll get out, the driver is trying to talk to us.' Some people screamed, some groaned, but we kept saying, 'shh, we'll get out, stay cool, the driver is talking to us, let's listen to him.'

The driver said, 'I've got to go forward a bit, then I can let you out, but first I need to make sure the track isn't live,' so we all shouted the message back into the darkness. It got passed down the train into the darkness. Then after about 20–30 minutes we started to leave the train.

It was choking on there so we were trying not to panic because we knew that would be curtains. We tried to keep each other calm, I remember saying 'if anyone's boss gives them grief for being late, we know what to say to them, eh, girls?' and people laughed. We kept saying 'not long, it's the long walk to freedom, nearly there'. I knew, if we panicked, we'd trip on the (possibly live) tracks and things would be hopeless. So we just tried to stay cool, and trust we'd be safe soon. We'd escaped from the smashed carriage, we just had to stay calm and escape from the dark tunnel too. We walked carefully through the semi-darkness – we didn't know if the tracks were live so we walked between them – the emergency lights were on in the tunnel – we walked in single file to Russell Square station and after what felt like half an hour we were lifted off the tracks to safety, and I was in a lift, euphorically calm, then in the station foyer, surrounded by filthy blackened shocked people, someone handing me water. My mouth was so dry. My lungs were full of choking dirt, it felt. I was aware then of a huge bleeding gash full of glass in my wrist and that I could see the bone in my arm, and I then felt sick. I realised I needed to clean it, it was full of grit, and I was bleeding, so I held my arm above my head and breathed in and out hard. But I also knew I didn't need an ambulance; it was a nasty gash, not a maiming. So I staggered about for a bit, outside the tube, and no one seemed to know what to do, least of all me, then I called my friend who worked in Shaftesbury Avenue and she came in a cab and she took me to the hospital.

We shouted, 'does anyone want to get a lift to the hospital?' but people seemed too shocked to respond, and I started to faint. I just wanted to get my wound cleaned and stitched and GET HOME, I was feeling sick and worrying much worse casualties would be coming later. In casualties I was 'walking wounded', not really badly hurt, and I felt almost bad for having survived and got off so lightly. I knew others behind me were so much worse off than I was. The hospital staff were so lovely, I kept wanting to cry. But I knew I needed to stay calm and get home. I got treated, my cut cleaned of glass and X-rayed – hours passed, I felt even more calm and light-headed – people started to flood into A&E at UCH covered in glass and blood.

The police talked to me and gave me a forensic bag for my clothes. I felt like I was out so fast and into hospital so fast the emergency services staff hadn't quite got geared up into 101 mode yet. I was so very lucky. The emergency staff were clearly shocked, yet doing all they could and rose to the occasion so bravely. I can't thank them enough. They were magnificent.

Anyway. They kept me in for four hours with shock, they stitched me up, then they wouldn't let me go, cos I had gone deaf and they weren't sure if I had broken my arm. X-rays proved it was just bashed. Eventually I got out and met my partner and walked to Camden (no buses/trains, desperate to get home). Seeing his face was wonderful. I started to shake with the relief of being alive.

In the pub I found out that there had been many bombs. I went into shock. I probably still am in shock. It took another two hours to get home; a friend eventually managed to pick us up in her car. I am very lucky. I feel euphoric. I'm sure I'll 'crash' soon, but right now, I'm so glad to be alive.

A S I WROTE I COULD feel some of the adrenaline draining away. This story, those screams, this smoke, leaving my pounding head, going into cyberspace, so anyone in London, anyone in the world could now read it and own it with me, come on the journey too. Before, it was a series of horrors beating at the insides of my skull, a fluttering horrible moth trapped in a dark, claustrophobic room, frantic to fly out into the night air. Now as I typed, it was released. I sat back in the chair, suddenly aching all over. My shoulders, my jaw, felt granite-hard with tension. I realised that my face was wet, with sweat, with tears. The disassociated numbness I still felt was a cold icy rock in my chest, it would take time to thaw and leave me. Meanwhile, what I felt, at last, was exhausted.

Almost immediately, people reading urban75 started to respond to my account. Somewhere in the city, people I did not know were reading what I wrote and reaching out to me. The extraordinary blessing of the kindness of strangers was manifesting itself again, people were writing back, my words reaching them at almost the speed of thought. The words on the computer screen swam in front of me; that was the tears coming again. People were sending me cyber-hugs, telling me to look after myself. I was so grateful and touched by their compassion. They were asking me for an update. I typed back.

> UPDATE 7 July 2005, 11.57pm
> I'm, okay, just starting to 'crash', I am keeping calm, but unable to get the horrible smell out of my nose, even though I have had a bath. I am getting a bit tearful, but I had this overwhelming need to get the story out, so everyone 'owned' it, and it wasn't just jammed in my head, freaking me out. It helps to say what happened. I'm grateful for the support.
>
> I'll keep in touch.

I THOUGHT THAT I COULD sleep now. I switched the computer off. I climbed back into bed, curled into J's warm back. I closed my eyes. I fell asleep. That night, I did not dream of anything at all. Another blessing.

CHAPTER FIVE

The day after the bombs

ALL OVER THE CITY, AS J lay sleeping, people were doing terrible work. At Edgware Road, Aldgate, Russell Square and King's Cross, Tavistock Square, forensic officers were investigating behind screens and barriers, more officers guarding the crime scenes. Just before midnight, as I turned off my computer, a police exhibits officer telephoned the investigators to say that along with many other personal items, cash and membership cards in the name of 'Sidique Khan' and 'Mr S Tanweer' had been found at Aldgate, and an investigation began, we were told later in the official Government Narrative, into the identity of these and other names, which included going through financial records. There was much to do, and down in the tunnels of the London Underground tube network was where the work was hardest.

They were fingertip searching among the remains. All

the passengers were gone now; they had cleared the tracks of those who were left behind, those who never completed their morning journey. The masked forensics officers in their white boiler suits were beach-combing on the shores of horror, gently, reverently, sifting for clues among the detritus of humanity left scattered after the atrocity. Handling it all with soft, gloved hands that were careful as a father with the limbs of a new-born baby, working in the stinking fetid darkness, illuminated with powerful lights so that the aftermath of all the brutality was exposed. On the walls of the tunnels, shadows moved. There was a whirr of generators in the stinking, airless tunnels, where the temperature rose and rose, causing the workers to run with sweat and their eyes to sting. 'I have seen hell,' said an officer to a journalist, who asked him about the scene of carnage he had emerged from; he would say no more. These men, these women, who walked back to the carriage from which I fled with the other commuters who could walk or be carried away, had now to become familiar with every inch of it. Where I could not bear to look, they must gaze for hours. They worked in short, appalling shifts: stooping, crouching under collapsing metal and rubble; carefully picking up wallets, newspapers, jackets, bags, umbrellas, coins, cards, socks, shoes, spectacles. And other things, things that were once human, once loved, still loved, now lost: body parts. Among them were the remains of the bombers, and the remains of their exploded bombs. I would call these workers more than brave: I would call them heroes.

There were so many individual acts of heroism on 7th July that I cannot record them all, and over a year later I know only a fraction of what people did on that day. I know some of what people did to help those on my train. I know of the London Underground staff of King's Cross and Russell Square, who saw the smoke emerging from the tunnel. They rushed into the tunnel to see what was happening; they went to help the passengers escape from the train. They were ordinary station staff, and a short while later, they were joined by the British Transport Police dedicated rapid response team who come when a train is trapped or when there is a person under a train, hurrying to save lives and tend the injured. Many of the London Underground staff first responders did not have time to ask permission from their managers to leave their work and enter the tunnel. They just ran, to guide the shocked and frightened passengers, who did not know (because there were no explanatory signs to tell them) that they could exit only through the last carriage or the front of the train; who, trapped, beat hopelessly at the closed doors and windows with bloodied hands as the black smoke filled the train and voices screamed with panic.

I know of the British Transport Police inspector, on duty at King's Cross with his colleague – keeping an eye out for protesters travelling to Scotland to demonstrate at the G8 summit – who heard the bang of the explosion on the Piccadilly line, felt it through the soles of his sturdy shoes. He went down to the platform and saw the smoke pluming out of the tunnel. He told his young newly qualified colleague to wait on the platform, and if he did not return, to seal the station and report him as 'missing'. Then he went into the tunnel to investigate, not knowing what he was going into, maybe a bomb, a chemical attack, a fire. He went in anyway, ignoring protocol, heading straight into unknown danger, and he squeezed his way up between the train and the tunnel wall, looking through the smashed windows that the frightened passengers had broken to let out the smoke, to let in the air, and he told the trapped people in the sixth, fifth, fourth, third, second carriages that somebody knew they were there, as he made his way up the tunnel. 'Ladies and gentlemen,' he called again and again, 'I am a police officer, and we are going to get you out as soon as we can.' Passengers who heard him told me later that this was the moment when they began to have some hope, when they realised that they were not going to die trapped underground, that rescue was on its way.

When the inspector got to the front of the train, to the carriage where the bomb was, he forced the buckled door into carriage one, and then he saw the extent of the devastation. He saw the splattered, shattered carriage walls, the hole in the floor, the hole in the roof, the missing doors, the blown-out windows, mangled metal, torn wires and smashed glass, and what else he saw, he told me, he would never speak of, 'out of respect for those people and their families'. Then he had to do something that he said 'went against all my moral fibre' and leave them, to turn back and get help. He promised them that he would summon help at once, and help came. In his nightmares, he told me once, he still returns to carriage one.

I know of the young station manager at Russell Square who saw on his screens that a train had stopped suddenly and who went to investigate. He too, went into the tunnel. He was one of the first to get to carriage one, the bombed carriage, where he found people who had been blown out of the train and were on the tracks. He took off his clothes and tore them to make tourniquets and bandages. I know of the driver who did not leave the train, who stayed and helped the injured while his co-driver, who had been travelling in the cab with him led the passengers who could walk, which included me, out from the front of the train to safety. I know of the fire service officers who went into the tunnel and who carried out the terribly wounded passengers, improvising make-shift stretchers out of coats and clothing strewn on the floor of the carriage, carrying them hundreds of metres down the tunnel to the platform at Russell Square, and then carrying them up flights of stairs to the station hall, because the lifts had stopped working, sweating, praying that they would make it. I know how many rescuers worried that the passengers they pulled to safety had later died of their injuries, despite their efforts; and a little of their joy when they found that some people they had rescued were miraculously still alive. I know these things now, because, they told me, over a pint, months later. But when I awoke on 8th July, I knew nothing of these things, because nobody had told me their stories.

WHEN I OPENED MY EYES on 8th July, I felt a dull pain in my wrist, smelled the tang of hospital disinfectant from the bandage on my wrist, next to my face on the pillow, and opened my eyes to sunlight, streaming through the gap in the cheap green curtains that had never fitted properly. I heard the slow breathing of Miff the cat; she was sleeping in a patch of sun on the carpet next to the bed. As soon as she heard me waking, she jumped onto the bed and pushed her head at my hands, making a small cheeping noise of desire, for food, for attention, eager to begin the small routines of her day. I sat up and looked at my hand; it was swollen and flecked with scores of little cuts, dark with the smoke from the tunnel. My nails and cuticles were still black, despite yesterday's bath. It didn't look like my hand; it looked like the hand of a much older woman. There was a sickly fire taste in my mouth, and a word came to me to describe it: *infernal*. I got up, leaving J still sleeping, and brushed my teeth, but afterwards the taste still remained, in my throat, my sinuses, my nostrils. I made some tea, left a mug for J next to the bed where he was still fast asleep, his arm thrown over his face. I opened the French windows from the bedroom onto our small back garden, slid back the metal security grille, which reminded me of the grille at Russell Square station, yesterday, the one that had kept the bombed passengers in the ticket hall and the commuters, and me outside. I noticed that my hand was shaking.

The cat followed me outside into the back yard, and weaved furrily round my ankles. I ignored her, because I wanted a moment here in the sunshine to think of where I was, what had happened and what might have been. Everything was very still.

There was a large bumblebee gathering pollen from a lavender bush in a cracked terracotta pot; I could see the pollen sacs on his legs, the hairs on them, the blur of his wings. I noticed that the bush needed watering. The air smelled of geraniums and warm earth. There was no wind, no traffic, no noise at all from the nearby terraced houses; no sound of TVs or radios, no splash of water as someone took a shower. My ears were still ringing, and they ached. I swallowed, to 'pop' the pressure but it made no difference. The only external noise was the bee, and the cat, crunching on the gravel, who had started to purr, and jump up at me, pushing against me with her strong soft body, telling me that she wanted her breakfast. I picked her up and tried to shush her – a big tabby cat, plush as a heavy cushion – but she would not be gentled, would not keep still on my lap, and so I gave up and carried her under my arm back into the flat.

As I fed her, I felt grateful to her for this small service she had done me of pushing my thoughts back to *now*, because as I sat on the bench, I had stopped noticing where I was. I could no longer feel the sun on my face, or smell the flowers. I had been falling backwards through yesterday, tasting the smoke, hearing the screams, the bang, going back underground, back into the tunnel. I shook my head, and stamped my feet, trying to dispel the lingering smoke, the sound in my ears. I wondered how many more people were waking up and wondering what had happened to them yesterday. The girl whose hand I had squeezed in the dark. The laughing black woman who had made us smile as she squeezed through the closing doors at King's Cross. The woman who had screamed and screamed after the bang, who had not been able to stop screaming. The man who had shouted to keep calm, that the driver was going to get us out. The driver who had helped me down the ladder into the tunnel. The shuddering woman with blood in her ears at Russell Square who could not meet my eyes. I wondered, as I stood barefoot in the kitchen, drinking tea that tasted of smoke, what had happened to all of the passengers from my train, where they were, if they were drinking tea in their kitchens now, if they had slept, if they were shaking like me, if they knew what had happened to them and whether I would ever find out any of their stories.

If this had happened ten years ago, there would be little chance of ever hearing from other survivors again. But now, there was every chance I could reconnect with fellow passengers. This was the age of multimedia communication, and like most people in the UK, I had an internet connection. I went to the study and switched on the computer, logging onto the message board where I had posted my story the night before. Unusually, the website editor had taken my story and put it in its own section of the website. There were now dozens of messages posted in response to my account. Many people wrote that they were crying. Some had sent me private messages. There was advice to rest, to talk to family and friends. One poster revealed that she worked for the London Ambulance service in the control room, and of how she had printed out the story I had posted of my journey and read it to staff there, and how it had made it real for them. She passed on best wishes from the Ambulance Control Room staff – and their thanks for taking a taxi to hospital. Another person gave me an extremely helpful piece of advice – to push a cold decongestant stick up my nose to get rid of the smell. Brilliant idea. I went to the bathroom cupboard and followed the advice. The infernal smell and taste disappeared. Then I blew my nose, hard, and coughed, and I looked at the tissue. It was black. The smell, the taste of the smoke was real; I wasn't going mad or being haunted by the tunnel after all, it was only because the smoke had got up my nose that I could smell and taste it all the time. I started to cry with relief, and gratitude that all these people whom I had never met were thinking of me and sending me hugs, prayers, thoughts and practical advice.

I typed a message back and posted it on the board:

Thanks everybody.

Sharing what happened helped.

I am feeling a bit hung over and my arm aches but apart from that am 90 percent fine. I was a bit traumatised and shocked yesterday and kept smelling the horrible smoke smell. Then I blew my nose and coughed a lot and it was black, so after that I felt better because I realised I wasn't going mad, the smell was real. And therefore would go in time. Especially if I put Vicks up my nose, good suggestion that. I am going back to work on Monday. Fuck the bombers. Just fuck 'em. I was so proud of London yesterday. I still am. Peddling hate-filled nihilistic claptrap is never going to get very far with us. I am still feeling glad to be here and glad to be alive and grateful to the emergency services, and the hero train driver, and the police. I'm going to sit in the garden today and look at the flowers and the sun and appreciate the hell out of everything.

My thanks: The police officers, CID forensic team, at UCH, the X-ray team, hospital support staff, doctors, nurses, the train driver, the volunteer nurse Faith who rushed in on her day off to man the outpatient ward, you were all absolutely wonderful and magnificent and I take my hat off to you. Thank you for looking after me. You stitched my wound, X-rayed me, cheered me and calmed me and cared for me. And hundreds of other frightened, hurt people. Big up to you.

T HOSE WERE ALL THE PEOPLE I had met yesterday.

J came into the study and put his arms around me and kissed the top of my head. 'How are you honey?' he asked. I stood up, hugged him, leaned onto his chest. 'I'm okay, I think.' I said, and I was. I was here, alive, almost unhurt, in his arms, and all around me were the thoughts and the kindness of strangers, all these people reaching out to me through words on a screen, a virtual village of fellow-Londoners to whom I felt connected because of their interest and kindness. This was London, my city, my people, and at that moment I had never loved London more. I felt small and safe in a friendly crowd who would catch me if I fell. I felt fortunate, more than fortunate, blessed.

Then I turned on the television. The national news was on. The announcer was saying that there were at least 50 people dead, and 'hundreds' wounded. He explained how many were believed to have died in each blast. Then he said that the bomb that had claimed most casualties was on the Piccadilly line, that it was the deepest part of the Underground, 70 feet below street level, and that it was a single track line – there was nowhere for the blast to dissipate as it could have in wider, shallower lines, so that was why there were so many fatalities. The announcer mentioned that an extremist Islamist organisation calling itself 'The Group of al Qaeda of Jihad Organisation in Europe' had claimed responsibility. It wasn't clear whether the claim was genuine or not, he said. I went back to the computer to see if I could find out more. On an American news website I found a translation of the claim of responsibility.

'*It is time of revenge against the crusader and Zionist*

British Government has come in response to the massacres committed by Iraq and Afghanistan.'

The grammar was peculiar, but perhaps it was a hasty translation from the Arabic. If the claim was genuine, then the attacks were carried out as 'revenge' for our foreign policy. I read on, feeling rising anger at the puerile posturing machismo of the language.

'*The mudjahadeen heroes have launched a blessed attack in London... Here is Britain burning now out of fear and horror in its north, south east and west. We have often and repeatedly warned the British Government and people... We still warn the Governments of Denmark and Italy and all the crusader governments that they will receive the same punishment if they do not withdraw their troops from Iraq and Afghanistan... We gave the warning, so we should not be blamed.'*

It was a vile piece of self-justification. '*We gave the warning, so we should not be blamed.*' But the news had said no warning had been received. And how could anybody claim they were 'heroes' for launching 'punishment' against ordinary innocent people travelling to work? We were not powerful, we were not politicians or people of influence. It was quite likely that large numbers of people on the train I had been on were against the war, had voted against the Government. Some of them were probably tourists from other countries, travelling to Heathrow. There were people of all ages and nationalities and religions using the tubes and the buses to get to work when the bombers attacked. Men and women and children, mothers and fathers and brothers and sisters, husbands and wives and lovers, best mates and house mates, colleagues, bosses, neighbours, and now more than fifty of them were murdered and hundreds injured, and these revolting idiots on this website were claiming that the bombers were 'heroes' for bombing them. They were no such thing: they were mass murderers. As for the idea that London, or Britain, was 'burning now out of fear and horror in its north, south east and west', that didn't sound very likely to me. Everyone I had met yesterday had been pretty calm. In fact, in the pub people had been extremely cheerful.

I went to the BBC website to see whether the terrorist fantasy of mass panic was borne out. I wanted to find out about the reaction of other Londoners. I especially needed to read the stories of the people who had been travelling on the same train as me. I found the page on the BBC news website with detail about the Piccadilly line bomb. Click.

And that was when I found out that I should have been dead.

The BBC website page said that the device was in the first carriage by the first set of doors where passengers stand. It said that the Picadilly line is 21.3 metres (70 feet) deep where the bomb exploded, and that rescue teams faced intense heat of up to 60°C, dust, fumes, vermin, asbestos, and that there were initial fears that the tunnel might collapse. A passenger was quoted describing the massive bang, the smoke everywhere and how hot it was, how everyone had panicked, started screaming and crying.

I STARED. BLINKED. READ IT again. There were the words on the screen, stating that the device was in the first set of double doors where passengers stand.

NO, THAT WAS WHERE I was standing. In the first carriage, by the first set of double doors.

On the website there was a graphic of the train – red, white and blue – and there was the first carriage, and there was the orange and yellow of the bomb explosion, by the first set of doors, exactly where I had stood. I looked at the picture, as my heart started beating faster and faster. The picture looked accurate, the train was the right colour, the right scale, yet I knew that it must be wrong, because otherwise, how could I possibly be alive? I found myself shaking, pacing about the room, then coming back and looking at the computer screen. I shouted at it. 'No. *No*. I'm *alive*, you are wrong, that wasn't how it was. It wasn't that close. It can't have been that close. *Don't you tell me that I should be dead. Don't you say it.*' And I heard the bang again, as if it were in the room, so loud that I flinched: there was a roaring in my ears and my mouth was numb, and the screen was blurred and I felt I was falling, that the ground had dropped away beneath my feet, and the room was spinning. I stopped pacing, my legs were going from underneath me, and J rushed in and grabbed me, and held onto me, and told me, 'Shush, baby, it's okay, you're here, you're alive, they must have made a mistake, you're white as a sheet.' And I said that they had made a mistake. 'They must have done. Otherwise I should be dead too.' And I burst into angry, frightened tears.

I cried for less than a minute, then I pulled myself together. Delayed shock. It struck me as odd that I had been so calm all day yesterday, and that I should be so spooked twenty-four hours later. But then, you don't expect to look at the BBC website and find out that you should be one of over fifty people who have been killed going to work.

My reality was dislocated. This was the BBC. The News. I had grown up trusting the BBC News more than I trusted God. The word of God was explained on a weekly basis in church by my dad, a vicar, who I knew could be proven wrong about things, but the BBC news was gospel. My childhood was punctuated by the sound of the beeps on the radio, then the authoritative voice of the newscaster, and my mother would pause, listen. 'Ssh, it's the News.' The sonorous voice on the kitchen radio announcing 'This is the *One O'Clock News* from the BBC' meant lunch. The *Six O'Clock News* meant homework. The *Today* programme meant getting ready for school. If the BBC said I had been standing where a bomb went off, then my immediate reaction was to believe the BBC and to doubt my own sanity and senses.

I sat down heavily at the computer desk. I was going to gather every memory I had and try and file them into some kind of order, as if I was the BBC news reporter. I wrapped my arms round my head, curling up, covering my eyes, took a deep breath, and let myself go back into the carriage. *BANG. Huge force smashing into my head and back, throwing me to the ground. Grinding of brakes. Train slowing down but still travelling fast, shaking violently. Like being on an out of control fairground ride, people screaming as if they are on a roller-coaster that is plunging too fast into a void, everything is dark, glass falling, bracing myself, can't see, can't breathe...*

Stop. I open my eyes. *That's enough.* I trust my memory

and what my body was telling me. The accurate report has come through. The bomb was definitely not by the first set of double doors, in the space between the seats where I and about fifteen others had been standing. It might well have been in my carriage – in fact – the more I thought about it, it must have been in my carriage, because that would explain the enormous violence of the bang – so loud that I could not hear it, the huge force that had thrown me forward to the floor, shattered the windows, smashed the lights, changed the stuffy carriage air which had smelled before of people's clothes, damp from the rain, into this horror of choking noxious smoke that was unbreathable, pouring down our throats, into our eyes, so I had thought I was blinded. At the time I had known the bomb was behind me – the force of it had thrown me forwards and sideways and onto the floor of the carriage – but I had thought the bomb to be further back on the train. I felt sick.

I decided to give up on the BBC for the time being. Instead I got a piece of paper and I drew a plan of the carriage, the doors and the seats and where I had been standing and exactly where I thought the bomb had been, based on the vivid flashback memories I had just experienced sitting in my chair. I put the paper carefully away in a drawer.

J was in the kitchen, making a cup of strong tea, the time-honoured British response to shock, terror and tears. I stayed in the chair, the computer screen switched to a screen-saver now; the picture of the bomb on the train which had distressed me, gone. My breathing and heart rate returned to normal. I stretched, thinking, while Miff leaned against my feet, doing a somersault and batting at my ankles with her paws. I was one piece of the jigsaw of the shattered journey. The bang shuddered through me still, the taste of smoke was still in my throat. Hundreds of other people had experienced the same thing with me. These strangers, fellow passengers whom I had never spoken to until the dark came upon us, the screaming started. What were they doing now? How many were in hospital? How many were watching, reading, listening to the news and also thinking, 'I should be dead?'

I clicked back on the message boards on urban75 to see if anybody had more information on where the bomb had been. The news from ordinary Londoners, published freely on the internet, minutes after the event, had become a more important source of information for me than the besuited figure behind the national news desk.

I was searching for what I later used as a definition of citizen journalism – *stories of the people, by the people, for the people*.

I didn't know then, but that was the moment when my life changed. I realised that I needed to write, more than anything else I had ever done, at 10.50am on the 8th July 2005, twenty-six hours after the bomb exploded and ten minutes after I realised that contrary to what the news said, the bomb had exploded in the middle of the carriage by the second set of doors. I had almost boarded there, but I'd changed my mind at the last moment and I got on at the first set of doors, where there was a little more space, because I had wanted to read my story. Telling my story and reading it in print on 7th July had saved my life. It meant I got on the first set of doors, not the second. Reading my account just before the bomb went off had kept me calm after the explosion; it had meant I was somehow prepared for the panic and sensory deprivation, because I was already pounding with adrenalin, in the soldier's combat 'zone' from reading about the rape attack. When I got home on 7th July, my reaction had been to write down the story. Telling my story of the bomb on the train had helped me, and now other Londoners reading had told me it had helped them too. Telling my story to myself again, trusting my memories had just calmed me down, taken me into the carriage then out again, and shown me that even the BBC could make mistakes. I had been close to the bomb, but not so close that I should have died. And my next reaction to the shattering news event of the London bombings was to look for other people's stories and to make sense of the political event through the personal narrative of ordinary people.

J put the tea in front of me, and kissed the top of my head. 'I'm going to phone the BBC,' I told him. It was the only thing I could think of to do to calm myself down. 'Fair enough,' he said. I called the BBC news desk and explained. The person taking the call was clear.

'That's where the police told us that the bomb was,' she said.

'But it wasn't there,' I said.

'We have to go on what the police tell us,' she said firmly. 'If you have different information then you need to tell the police.'

'Okay,' I said, 'do you have a number for the police? The police who gave you the information about where the bomb was?'

'No,' she said. She sounded like she didn't believe me. I wanted to shout at her. *This is all true, I am not going mad.*

'But please, you understand,' I said, 'that if the police think the bomb was at the front of the train, then they won't be going into the train the right way to get the bodies out? You can go in the front via Russell Square, you can go straight in, that is how we got off, the tunnel is ok there...'

'You should call the police,' she said again. I gave up, thanked her, hung up.

I had no idea which police to speak to. The news was giving out a casualty hotline number, but that didn't sound like the right number to call, presumably that was for people trying to find out about missing loved ones. But I couldn't bear the thought of the wrong information being out there, people freaking out like I just had done, the police going into the train from the wrong end.

J called out from the sofa, 'There's an anti-terrorist hotline on the telly, quick.' I grabbed a pencil and wrote the number on the back of an envelope, then called it straight away. I started to explain what I had tried to tell the BBC person.

'Woah, steady,' she said, 'so you were on the train? Which train?'

I told her. The Piccadilly line, the first carriage, going from Finsbury Park to Covent Garden via King's Cross.

'Carriage one? First carriage?' she asked. 'Whereabouts?' I started gabbling, desperate to pass on what I knew, trying to give her my exact position. 'I got on at the first set of doors, first carriage, the doors on the left, I was standing in the middle, near the pole, towards the second set of seats, not the first, on the same side as the first set of left-hand doors, then I fell forwards, towards the first set of double doors on the left of the train as you faced direction of travel, we escaped out the front, down the ladder...'

'Hang on, it's fine, I'm going to listen to all of this, but first I need to take your details,' she said kindly, then took my name, address, date of birth, telephone number, repeating them back to me. She let me tell her everything, then thanked me. 'I'm going to ask some officers to come round to interview you,' she said, 'you've been very helpful, well done, will you be in over the next few days?'

I said I didn't think I was in a mad rush to go anywhere particularly.

'No, well, that's very sensible. Have you got someone who can look after you?' I said I was fine, my boyfriend lived with me. She told me that she'd ask the officers to ring me and tell me when they were coming over. I said thank you, and hung up. She believed me. The relief was enormous. I sat down next to J on the sofa and he put his arm round my shoulders and kissed me. 'Good girl,' he said. 'Now drink your tea.'

The tea was cold, but I drank it anyway. It was one of several dozen mugs of tea that I was to drink over the next few days. The morning passed hazily watching the news. I was alternatively pounding with anger and adrenalin, then feeling falling-over tired. The phone kept ringing, and I spoke to my family and friends, more texts kept arriving. I told everyone, again, and again, *I'm all right, don't worry about me, it's ok.* Several beautiful bunches of flowers arrived over the course of the day. I trimmed their stems and put them all in buckets to have a long drink, sniffling because I felt so overwhelmed by support and love and I didn't know what to say to people. *Thank you for being happy that I am still alive.* J went out to get the papers, and came back with a pile of them, all full of the same news, horror, outrage, pictures of flowers, people weeping, Tony Blair looking stony-faced, diagrams of the trains, the mangled bus, the same pictures, over and over again. I would read them and start shaking, then put them down when the words started to shimmer and swim in front of my eyes. Listen to the news, feeling numb, feeling nothing inside but spinning nausea. My stomach kept flipping, and I kept coughing and retching up the tea. I splashed one mugful down my front, then dropped the next on the floor. I paced about and walked into things and banged myself, but didn't feel any pain. Two journalists rang, wanting to come round and take pictures and interview me. I couldn't think of how they had managed to get my number, unless that woman in the café had been from a news agency. I told them no. Then the woman from the café rang back, asking for a follow-up interview.

'We'd like to re-interview you, can you be ready in half an hour? We'll send a car, what's your address?'

I said no thanks, I was just resting now. She was insistent. 'We'll send a makeup artist, who'll do your hair and makeup,' she said. 'You'll look fabulous!'

I said I had no interest in having a make-over, thank you, I was just pleased that I was alive and having my hair blow-dried for free seemed rather beside the point right now. She started to say something about money. I got fed up and asked her to leave me alone. She went away with bad grace, and ten minutes later she called back again. 'We'll give a donation to charity, if you prefer,' she said, 'or you can go on a little holiday, wouldn't that be a nice rest? Now we need you to...'

I felt my cheeks growing hot. 'Will you just stop, please?' I said, my voice rising to an indignant squeak. '*Leave me alone. People have died and you're talking about bloody holidays?'* I looked at the news, which was showing a young blonde woman, her beautiful face swollen with tears, holding a 'missing' photo of a young man outside a station; behind her lay dozens of piles of flowers. I snapped the mobile phone shut, cutting off the reporter. Hanging up was the height of rudeness. Well, too damn bad.

J looked at me, turned the news off, took the phone away from me and led me outside into the yard.

'Sit down, for God's sake,' he said, pushing me firmly onto the bench, and went back into the house, returning with a tumbler full of whisky. He sat next down to me, and held my knee as I drank all the whisky obediently. The anger at the insensitive reporter was gone, and I felt numb again, and ashamed of my temper. The phone rang again. It was my sister. 'How are you?' she asked, her voice full of concern.

'Fine. How are you?' I said, limply. 'I'm just sitting in the garden.'

'I'm coming over,' she said.

'You don't have to,' I said, feeling guilty. 'It's nothing, I'm fine. Completely fine, just got a bit of a cough. Don't worry.'

J took the phone off me, and spoke to Anna, rolling his eyes at me as he talked. 'Ignore your silly big sister. Come on over.' Anna said she'd be round at tea time. I realised then it was almost four o'clock. The day had passed in a surreal blur of cups of tea, and beautiful flowers, and horrible, still-unbelievable news.

Clouds passed over the sun, their shadows moved over the garden and I stared at the ivy on the roof of the falling-down garage at the end of the yard. The whisky had smothered up the smoke-taste in my mouth. I was cold. My arms were covered in goose-pimples, not from the temperature, but from a sense of evil outrage poisoning the summer afternoon. I looked down at my black claws. I wanted to go into the bathroom and cut the nails down as short as I could, scrubbing them with a nailbrush until they were red and raw, but clean, only I was too tired to start looking for the nail cutters. My hands were still lined with grey marks, but they were starting to look like my own hands again, and I covered my face with them, tried to cry, but no tears would fall.

Later that day, after my sister Anna had stepped through the door and enfolded me in a huge hug, the wild euphoria kicked in again, and the shaking stopped. This was partly due to the quarter pint of whisky I drank over the next few hours. We watched a programme about baby elephants, briefly felt normal delight, talked about Anna's job. Pizza arrived, and I ate it ravenously, the first food I had eaten in a day and a half. Afterwards, my stomach was swollen as I had bolted the greasy food, and I started to nod my head forwards, eyes, heavy, sinking into the warmth of semi-sleep where I was, curled on the sofa. My boyfriend and my sister talked in low voices, as I dozed. I fell asleep for a few hours, blankly unconscious and snoring, until J shook my arm, told me to go to bed, and Anna bent and kissed me goodnight and left for her flat in South London. In a taxi. She had wanted to get the tube, I was too tired to argue and try to stop her. J insisted, and I was more glad and relieved than I could say.

But as soon as I lay down on the bed, still feeling nauseous and utterly drained, I was wide awake again. I would close my eyes, and the darkness would come, bang, screams, and I then would jump up again, eyes stretched, heart thundering. This went on for over an hour until I was almost whimpering with fatigue. I got up, and found a bottle of herbal sleeping tablets. Although the recommended dose was two tablets, I took four. It worked within fifteen minutes; I calmed down. Although I still felt sick with a trickling cold fear of what I might dream about, I managed to let go of the tension in my body enough to trust that sleep would come, and though I heard the bang, and the grinding brakes once more as I dropped off, sleep came. In the morning, I didn't remember whether I had dreamed or not, as everything since yesterday morning had the disorientating strangeness of a waking dream.

CHAPTER SIX

Lucky

SATURDAY MORNING FELT MUCH MORE normal. Though the wooziness of exhaustion was still there, the adrenalin dump that had left me shaking all Friday had almost passed. I spent an hour in the bath, the muscles in my legs and shoulders aching. I hacked my black toenails and fingernails off with kitchen scissors and massaged rose cream into my battered hands and cut feet. The last tiny piece of glass floated out of my ears as I lay with my head underwater and it disappeared down the plughole as the water drained away. My chest still felt full of soot and crackled when I breathed out. The stitches on my wrist, which I tried to keep dry, were already healing up, the deep laceration crunchily scabbing over. J had gone out to buy milk. Everything would be fine, I told myself as I went to the computer again, to tell everyone it was going to be okay, not to worry; to reassure myself by writing it, as much as others. To see if there was any news, anywhere, of any of the other passengers on the train. The last faces I saw before the bomb – had they survived? The laughing woman with the beautiful braids – had the bomber got on behind her? *Was she all right?* And I needed to check about the position of the bomb. How close it had been. Find out why I wasn't dead.

As I switched on the computer, I was wondering whether I was going to get PTSD, post-traumatic stress disorder, again – the psychological injury caused by the unprepared mind being overwhelmed by the threat of imminent death. The strange invisible wound I had struggled with after the rape, that had blighted my sanity, numbed my emotions, left me trapped in a cycle of juddering over-reaction to innocent stimuli, and gasping after horrified replays in my dreams. A toxic frozen hinterland of shadows, fear and depression and impotent rage, where I had been condemned to wander as a lost soul, looking at the world through an invisible membrane. Breathing in my own sickness, Untouchable.

Oh well, at least I knew the drill, if it happened again, I told myself, biting the inside of my cheek and tasting the copper tang of blood. It was too early to do much about it now, but maybe I should go and book a massage or see a counsellor or something. I was too damn tired to worry about it, though. *I'm talking to people who love me, I'm writing it down, and I'm all right. I'm not going to go under. Not this time. I know how to escape, read the signs, out-run the fear. This time you will not be able to touch me.*

I thought of WH Auden's poem, 'Musée des Beaux Arts', about the banality of evil, which had haunted me years ago.

'About suffering they were never wrong, The Old Masters;

how well they understood its human position; how it takes place/While someone else is eating or opening a window or just walking dully along…'

I remembered the line '*…the dreadful martyrdom must run its course*'. And *'How everything turns away/Quite leisurely from the disaster…'*

'Musée des Beaux Arts' from *Selected Poems* by W. H. Auden, published by Faber and Faber (reprinted with kind permission of Faber and Faber Ltd).

Nobody was turning away from the atrocity now; it was on every news channel, every newspaper and radio station. But it had taken place largely unseen. People above ground had been hurrying along, starting their ordinary working Thursday when it had happened. Queuing for buses, buying their croissants and toast and their paper cups of tea and coffee. Picking up the free newspapers full of the news of the Olympics win, and the G8 talks about making poverty history, and the hopeful future we might one day have. And beneath the streets, commuters and workers and tourists and students had been dying, ordinary innocent people horribly injured and trapped and crying in the dark for help. And almost nobody had known what had happened. Not until the bus had exploded – the fourth rucksack having been detonated by the lumpish teenager from Bradford – did people begin to know of the devastation caused by these 'martyrs', these maimers, these mass-murderers.

At the time I did not know the biographies of the killers, nor that they had died detonating their bombs. I knew that the killings had been linked to Islamist extremists; I knew that suicide bombing was being speculated about and I simply could not get my head around it. I lived in an area of London that was full of Muslim families; many of the local shops and businesses were Muslim-owned. I loved the area; sometimes it felt like being in North Africa or the Mediterranean rather than North London. I liked shopping at the food shops with their bunches of fresh coriander and mint, their piles of mangoes and figs and fat grapes, spiced olives in golden oil and fresh salty goat cheese that I would clap into still-warm bread from the Turkish bakeries. I liked the buzz in the streets on a Friday night after prayers at the mosque, when dozens of people would crowd outside the coffee shops and buy sticky pistachio pastries to take home for their families. Women in headscarves and flowing dresses were a common sight, as were crowds of chattering young men heading for Finsbury Park Mosque, a large building a few minutes' walk down the road. *Oh God, save us from a stupid anti-Muslim backlash; I don't want my London at war with itself.* But I told myself not to panic.

The murderers wanted us to be too scared to go on buses and trains. They wanted tourists not to come, people to be terrorised, cowering and terrified. Maybe the last bomb's location had been deliberately chosen to provide a camera-friendly moment of destruction; the iconic red bus, mangled, was the signal meant to shock and sicken us, create the immediate selfish thought, 'But that happens in Baghdad, not *London.*'

How did they think that frightening people would lead to the achievement of the UK becoming a Sharia state? How could it? There was no intelligent strategy behind this; it achieved *nothing.* Was their aim to stir up race hate, faith hate, and thus recruit more nihilistic young fools to their stupid death cult? If so, I thought, that had backfired as well. Muslims had died too on those trains and that bus; killing all those people in London was not going to save a single Muslim life or stop a single bullet being fired anywhere in the world. They had brought shame on themselves, those men with their bombs, and shame on the religion in whose name they claimed to act on that hideous website message. They were not proper Muslims; they were murderous death fetishists, disgusting criminals. I hoped that the police caught them soon, and that they were forced to explain their stupid reasoning for their actions, and that they would soon see how they were despised and condemned, how they had brought shame, not honour, on their faith and their families. And the best way to defeat such fools, I wrote determinedly on the message board, later that day, is to go to work on the tube, to dress and work how I want as a woman, to enjoy the rich social life that London has to offer, to have no fear of my neighbours, though they might come from other cultures, other creeds. Only to be wary of the hateful, the hate-filled, the nihilistic, the furiously angry, those whose words and bodies were weapons and who would not listen, could not engage. Men whose worlds had shrunk to their own selfish egos, their own cruel desires, men without pity, without empathy, without humanity. Men like that young man who had launched himself through my door a few years ago, and taken out his anger on me with his fists and his feet and his teeth. There was no point trying to reason with someone like that. You might as well try and argue with an axe that was being thrown at you. You could only try to get out of the way and hope that the violence would not finish you off. But men like that are thankfully rare. I thought the terrorist

101

bombers were probably like the rapist: common criminals, selfish and self-justifying. Nobody sane would listen to them; nobody normal would be anything other than repelled by their actions. There would be no race war, no hate attacks. *It would all be all right.*

I almost believed what I wrote. I wanted to believe it. I was trying very hard to convince myself that sanity would prevail. I knew we would cope, that London would cope, but I was still afraid. Not of my neighbours, not of Muslims, but of the young men who had done this, and why they had done this, and the bloody mess we were in, as a species, here at the beginning of the twenty-first century. The hate and the anger and the aggression that were everywhere, the fact that we were still at war after a twentieth century of 'wars to end all wars', and that hate and violence were still infecting everything. I thought of the angry drunk man in the pub on Thursday night, 7th July, whom I had met on the way home from hospital. And I remembered how he had cried.

I was angry, but I wanted to cry too. I went out instead, to buy some stuff for a Turkish breakfast: melon, soft white bread, feta cheese and sweet orange tomatoes. I bought the papers, all of the tabloids and the broadsheets. And another copy of *Marie Claire* magazine with the rape story in, to replace the copy that I had dropped on the tube. The anxiety I had felt about that article coming out and reliving the rape seemed years and years ago.

I was lying on the sofa with J, surrounded by piles of newspapers, stroking his hair while he talked to me of how he felt about all this madness, when the police rang to say that they would like to come round and interview me. They arrived a few hours later, two men, both Metropolitan Police detectives, fatherly and kind in their manner, and I made them a cup of tea. We sat at the table in the garden and I asked them how many statements they had taken. They said that they had been working pretty much non-stop, everyone was flat out. They told me that they normally worked on Operation Trident stuff, guns and gang crime. They admired the peacefulness of the garden and laughed at Miff, who was rolling in the dust and showing off her fat, spotted belly. They said that they hoped I would be all right to go through it all, that we could take our time. I said it would be fine. But please, did they know, please, could they tell me where the bomb had been. Because I really, really needed to know. I said that I had a diagram of where I was sure that it had been, and that I thought that the BBC was wrong. I took the paper out of my pocket and began to unfold it to show them. They looked at each other.

'Why do you think the BBC was wrong?' asked the slightly older detective, whom I will call Bill.

'Because they put the bomb by the first door in the first carriage,' I explained. 'Only, it can't have been there. Otherwise, I would be dead.'

They both looked at me, and then the younger officer, whom I will call Dave, said gently, 'Well, we'll definitely need to have a look at that later, but we need to go through the whole journey in chronological order, and not tell you what we know, or we'll be putting ideas in your head, and that will affect your witness account, and we'll be in trouble.' And he smiled at me, but I could see the anxiety and the tired shadows round his eyes. Then they got out a lot of paper and pens and we began, starting with my name, age, occupation and date of birth. Then the whole journey in laborious detail from when I had got up and dressed and what clothes I had worn. Whom I remembered seeing, where I had stood, descriptions of everything, what time I had thought it was. They remarked that my memory of the journey was hazy from Finsbury Park to Caledonian Road, then once we got to King's Cross the account changed and it suddenly got very clear with a high level of detail. I explained that I had been reading the magazine very intently and when I finished the article I had become very alert and focused, and how I had begun noticing everything.

'Why do you think that was, then?' asked Dave, looking genuinely interested. Beneath their avuncular manner, and despite their obvious tiredness, they were very sharp and alert. I was impressed. I went and got them the magazine and showed them the article about me being attacked, and explained how I had been reading it, lost in remembering it all. How afterwards I had managed my anxiety and claustrophobia by concentrating on everything around me. They looked at the feature, and the picture (which was cropped, but you could see it was me if you were standing next to me) in silence for a minute, and Bill scratched his head with his pen. 'Christ,' he said. And then apologised.

I said that I needed some water and asked them if they would like some more tea, and they said water would be great, ta. I left them for a few minutes and went into the kitchen so they could look at the magazine article and not have to ask me questions about it. When I came back Dave asked me how I would describe what it was like in the carriage as the doors closed at King's Cross, and I told him about the crush, the lady who had laughed as she came through the doors, and all the faces and voices and details I could remember. And then I had to tell them about the train leaving the station and how far I thought it had travelled before the explosion.

They asked if I wanted a rest 'before the bad bit coming up', and I said no, and then I told them. Everything about when the bomb went off, and everything that had happened afterwards, and where I had stood, where I had been thrown forwards when the blast happened. Bill wrote it all down, and afterwards I saw that he was pale and sweating. So I asked him if he was all right. It turned out that Bill was a diabetic, and he hadn't eaten. He asked if I had some orange juice. I rushed off and got him some, and a plate of biscuits, and he apologised and drank the juice and looked better. Dave looked a bit pale as well so I made him have a biscuit. We must all have looked completely knackered, but we smiled at each other and made jokes all the same.

We carried on with the rest of the statement, with Bill shaking his hand whenever it got cramped, and then we finally finished, and I read it back, and signed all the pages. Dave asked if they could take away all the clothes that I had been wearing on the train. I had put them all in the brown paper sacks that the police had given me at the hospital. But I didn't want to let them go.

I looked recalcitrant. 'Do I have to? They're new. They're the best clothes I have, I've only just bought them.' Bill blinked and looked tiredly at me. I immediately felt guilty. These guys were shattered; they didn't have time to waste politely persuading me to hand over my suit for forensic investigation. We had been working on this statement for over four hours. This was a murder case. I felt ashamed of my selfishness, and resigned myself to saying goodbye to my new suit, my favourite red sandals, my new linen blouse still with its tag in, bought for the first big presentation of my new job last Thursday. 'Do you want my umbrella too?' I asked, remembering how it had been drizzling.

'Was it open? There might be some goodies…'

'No, it was rolled up.'

'Don't worry about it then.'

I handed over the bags of reeking clothes, and they sealed them. The smell made me feel faint. I forgot to ask Bill and Dave if they wanted my handbag, so I never handed that over. It was new, too, bought a fortnight ago, part of my new Grown Up Advertising Director wardrobe for the new job. Now it sat in the study, sticky and blackened and full of glass.

I took a deep breath. 'Can I ask about the bomb now? Where it was?'

Dave said yes, and Bill asked me to sit down. I suddenly felt afraid.

'Hang on, can I get J?'

'Good idea.'

I went and found J on the sofa, and asked him to come into the garden. He was watching *Sky Sports*, but he came at once and sat at the fourth chair at the garden table, holding my hand. I noticed that the sparrows were making a huge racket in the ivy on the garage roof, and that the cat was on the wall, crouching and staring intently at them. Over the garden fence drifted the smell of barbecuing meat and the sound of cheerful voices chattering in a different language, one I didn't recognise. I pushed the diagram I had drawn over to Bill and Dave, and they looked at it. Then Dave reached into a black briefcase and drew out a folded piece of paper, which he consulted.

'You're right. Absolutely right. You are an – amazingly – lucky, lucky girl. The bomb was in your carriage, by the middle doors, pretty much right behind you, as far as I know.'

Then they told me what they knew. And J held my hand so tightly it left white marks on my skin. And I thanked them, and they thanked me, and I showed them to the door and they drove away. I went back into the house and joined J, who was still outside, and I tried to take it in. That I was alive because the carriage had been so crowded, that others had taken the full force of the bomb.

We stood in the garden in silence, holding each other, listening to the bees in the lavender bushes. My mouth felt numb.

We looked at each other and we talked of those who were missing and the people who had been standing behind me. I thought again of the terrible screams. The man covered in blood who was being half carried, half dragged by the man walking behind me on the tracks to Russell Square. He had groaned all the way while we were walking in single file to the tube. I thought of how the other passengers had died. Whether they had time to know what had happened.

I had a dizzying sense of vertigo, as if I had stepped back from a sheer cliff and the ground had rushed up to meet me. I went back into the flat and found the BBC news website and I looked again at the diagram of the carriage and the bomb. I could not stop staring at it. Then I looked at the diagram in the *Times* of the tunnel and the carriages and the bomb and the little escaping people, making their way down the tunnel to safety.

I still could not see why I was alive and had escaped with just a cut arm and scratches. J held me while I asked him this question, over and over again, and he stroked my face, and he had no answer for me.

Then he told me that Jane, our neighbour and one of my best friends, had asked us to come over for supper. I thought about it, another ordinary Saturday night with a friend. I thought of all the people who had made weekend plans on Thursday, and for whom everything had changed, because now they were in hospital, or at the bedside of someone they loved, or who were sitting at home grief-stricken, because someone had not come home. I didn't know what to do. What was the right thing?

I poured myself an enormous whisky. It didn't make me feel drunk, but it made me feel normal. I put on lipstick. We went out of the house together. It was a beautiful night, warm and soft and I could smell garlic cooking, and the scent of flowers.

The streets seemed quieter than normal, the usual crowds of young men who hang around outside the cafés of Finsbury Park were not there. J and I held hands tightly, and walked to meet Jane in a nearby bar.

And when we got there, suddenly a wave of joy hit me, and none of us could stop talking, and smiling at each other. I looked at the street outside, the trees, the shops and the people walking about, and I loved them all. We left the bar and picked up some wine from the off-licence, and I found myself beaming at the Turkish shopkeeper as if he were a favourite uncle. He looked bemused but smiled back.

We sat in Jane's garden, downing glass after glass of cold white wine and eating mango salad that her next door neighbour brought round, all of us babbling with happiness – and getting completely drunk.

I walked home again, still holding J's hand and I fell into bed at 3.00am, saying to myself again and again, 'I'm alive. I'm really alive, I'm still here.' Hugging myself. Realising finally how lucky I was. In among all the guilt, the fear, the miraculous fact that I was breathing, still living my ordinary life had passed me by.

Until this sweet moment. Until now.

CHAPTER SEVEN

The bomb journals

ON SUNDAY MORNING I WOKE up, still in a disbelieving state, mildly hung over, with the sun once more pouring through the curtains. J lay sleeping, his arm thrown over his face, the cat nesting at the foot of the bed, snoring. I made myself a cup of tea and took an armful of yesterday's newspapers into the garden. I read page after page of horror, maiming, death and analysis. I read of the anguish of those looking for the missing, the moderated outrage of politicians and the tight, tired statements of the police. Despite the nausea burning the back of my throat, there was still that floating-with-happiness, dislocated feeling. I wondered at myself; *why am I reading the news all the time? I already know what happened.*

I felt disgusted with my own reactions.

I had been shocked, I knew, and my reactions had yet to

reset to normal, but still, it felt ghoulish. I had cried only once, and that was with surprise and selfish anger and fear at hearing that I had been standing where the bomb had been. I did not think I could bear to cry properly yet. I supposed it would happen in time.

I went back to the computer to post an update on urban75, since so many people had asked yesterday what happened next, telling me to keep in touch. I reflected that my life had become a soap opera delivered in instalments. But I was needily, greedily grateful for people's good wishes and kindness.

Among the many private messages left for me by this kindly community of London-based website surfers was one from another poster who said that he worked for the BBC. He wrote that he had been following my diary, and had shown it to BBC colleagues, and they would like 'to share it with a wider audience'. Would I like to write a diary for the BBC for a week?

Blimey.

I thought about it, remembering how I had searched for stories like mine all weekend, ever since the bomb happened. Now the BBC wanted my story and people looking for the story of the bombed train would have at least one account of the bomb and after, from a fellow passenger. I sent a message to Mike, the editor of urban75, asking if it was alright to move my account to another site, offering to mention urban75 in the copy. Mike wrote back that of course it was fine and good luck. So that was settled: I was a writer for the BBC for a week, writing unpaid, as what was later called a 'citizen journalist'. I toned down the swearing, and the politics, which

I surmised might be fine in the sometimes-anarchic environs of the online urban75 community, but would not sit well with the neutral BBC, and I sent off my first piece. Within half an hour, it and the original messages posted straight after the bomb appeared on the BBC website, described as the diary of 'R, from North London, a survivor of the Piccadilly line bomb'. No photo, only an image of commuters crowded onto a packed Piccadilly line train, whose faces could not be discerned. I wanted to be anonymous; this was not just my story; it could have been the story of anyone on that train.

I wrote what I called to myself 'the bomb journal' every day, pausing only to check my spelling. The words flowed easily, effortlessly. I did not stop to think of the consequences of making my private thoughts so public, since I was nameless, faceless and nobody knew who I was or where I lived. In any event, after nearly dying on the way to work, very little seemed of any consequence; nothing seemed to matter very much at all. I rattled out my hopeful, heartfelt diary emails to Gary, the UK news editor of *BBC Online*, whom I had never met face to face. Sometimes I wrote several entries a day, pouring out the shock and my sadness and my gratitude to be alive; and he posted them straight up on the site, unedited, and out they went into the world. I trusted, without thinking about it, that all would be well, and that I would continue to be lucky and safe and protected from harm. And I was fortunate indeed, because mostly, that was how it turned out.

The writing had become healing, a way to talk myself through the hours and days of a strange summer week where nothing made sense. The words flowed out of me after the bomb in a way that words had not done for years. I had written like this as a child, easily, fluently, unselfconsciously. I had kept a journal as a teenager and co-written several books with a school friend, full of stories, poems, gossip, illustrations, that had been passed around our classmates. Later, I had gone on to study English at university, and faced with the dance and dazzle of the world's best wordsmiths as a daily diet, my ability to write had shrivelled in shock, like a feeble green shoot blasted by the brighter and better light of the literati. I put my schoolgirl scribbling away, chastened. It took a bomb going off for me to switch off the critical voice that started up whenever I wrote, which said, *'What do you know about anything, hopeless fool? Not much,'* I thought, as my fingers skittered over the keyboard. *'But I know about this, because I was bloody well there, so you can shut up and let me write about it, for once.'* And the inner critic was silenced.

Writing for myself had become a lifeline; writing for other people was also a great comfort. Alone at a desk in a small, scruffy study, I was still wide-eyed with shock and sufficiently numbed to no longer care much about the future, only the *now*, since I could not tell from one moment to the next how I was going to feel and what I was going to remember and re-experience. Sometimes I would be half mad with a peculiar joy, caught in the moment of watching the cat bat at a bee, or gazing at J's eyelashes flutter as he slept. Other times I would be enveloped in a phantasmal darkness, retching up sour bile and feeling the bang of the bomb again and again, tasting the smoke even though I was in a bright room with the TV showing a nature documentary and pasta cooking on the stove. Writing was a way of releasing the demons, the madness and despair that can bend the shocked brain out of shape and fracture the sense of safety and self after too-close horror. When I was writing I did not feel alone; though the audience was faceless, intangible, nonetheless I could feel a connection with those compassionate strangers. Through that hopeful pull of other people's presence, further along the path ahead towards the light of normality, encouragement sensed and read in other peoples' written responses, I could feel it and find it: a way out of the tunnel.

The BBC bomb journal was a week of wincing and small wonders. On Monday, after a comical visit to my GP to check my stitches, where I had to tell the doctor to pull herself together as she started flapping with shock, I returned to the computer to find a message from a man named Mark. He had found my account on urban75, and had registered with the website community to send me a message that he had been on the same train. He lived up the road, ten minutes' walk away, and he had travelled in my carriage, a few feet away from me. It had been his voice in the darkness that I had heard calling out that it was all right, the driver was going to lead us off the train. That was the message I had in turn tried to pass on to try to halt the panic and screaming around us. Because of that communication, about twenty-five of us had managed to keep calm and walk to safety from the front of the train. Mark's story of the bomb going off exactly matched my story. I invited him and his wife Sarah to come over for some wine. He accepted, said he could come tomorrow as he too had to visit the doctors – and then he told me something that gave me a great leap of hope. He had already got back on the tube.

When we finished talking, I immediately sent a text to my boss and told her that I would be coming back to work, too, on the tube. But please could I come in late and avoid the rush hour?

So the next day, Tuesday, I prepared to set off, with a watery feeling in my stomach and a shaky feeling in my chest. I carried my heels in a bag, and wore flat shoes, in case I needed to run. And a bottle of water, which I normally carried in hot weather. I had forgotten the water on 7th July, but I did not think I would ever forget again. I decided that the way I would manage the tube was to think about getting out the other end, and how pleased I would be when I did so. And of how much I liked my new job, which I had only started in May. Being a terrorism survivor was not the way I wanted to raise my profile in the office. I needed to get back to work and back to normal, as soon as possible. I told J that I would look at the other passengers, and if I started to have a panic attack I would just have to break Londoners' famous unwritten rule – 'Don't Talk We're On A Tube' – and ask for help. And if I saw anyone leaving their bag unattended, I thought I would probably slap them.

'I'm coming in with you,' said J.

'You'll be late for work,' I said.

'I don't give a stuff, you goose,' he said. 'And if my boss does, I'll probably slap *him*.'

Which made me laugh and helped enormously. And off we went to Finsbury Park station.

As we got there, though, I saw that the station staff had closed the grille and were no longer letting people into the station. People were milling about trying to get onto the Victoria line train. The Piccadilly line was closed: it would remain closed for four weeks while the police forensic team worked on the murder scene. It turned out, when J asked one of the station staff, that the Victoria line was closed due to station over-crowding. And I had waited and waited to come in, hoping that it would be a quiet part of the day, because I knew I could not face another overcrowded train. I almost burst into tears. It brought back unwelcome memories of the crush on the Piccadilly line train before the bomb, of Russell Square station grille being closed as I and other survivors staggered about trying to get out of the station into the fresh air.

'Do you want to get a cab, honey?' asked J, looking concerned. I said no. 'I won't be able to have you next to me next time I get onto the tube, and I've got to get on it, otherwise it will just get worse and worse.'

We went and had a coffee and I began to sniffle with frustration and fear. I didn't want to get on at all: I wanted to go back home, very badly, but I knew I had to do it, and the delay was making it much harder.

We paid for the coffees, and I called work again to let them know that I was still trying to get to work. Then I pressed my lips together and walked to the platform, turning left to the Victoria line instead of right to the Piccadilly line, as I had done last time.

And I got on the first carriage, by the first set of double doors, just as I had done on Thursday. But this time, I got a seat.

As the train set off I began to well up and shake. I held J's arm tightly. As we approached King's Cross, a pale-faced man in his forties sitting opposite me, wearing a suit and a black tie, leaned forwards. 'Is this your first time back on the tube?' he asked, having noticed my distress and looking a little shaky himself.

I said yes.

'Were you...?'

'Yes... were you...?'

His name was Eamon; he worked as a buyer in a large department store. We had both been on the same train on Thursday. At that point I recognised his face, from the newspapers and from the TV news. We talked of how frightened we had been. Our words tumbled out in a rush and the journey passed quickly. We exchanged numbers, and shook hands as I left the train. I surfaced at Oxford Circus, with J, in tears of relief and amazed yet again that I had met another survivor.

J kissed me goodbye, and headed off to his office. I arrived at work and sat down to catch up with my boss who was sympathetic and kind. My team were glad to see me. Cups of tea all round. I couldn't concentrate much on work, though I had meetings with my team and passed on details of ongoing pitches, meetings in the diary, made some handover notes. I didn't feel much of a hotshot account director, more like a nervous new intern. But I was glad to be back in the office, and my colleagues said that they were glad I was there too.

That night, Mark and Sarah came round to visit J and me – strangers who were neighbours, who had suddenly become friends, because of the bomb. They brought a plant as a gift. Mark had small cuts, grimed with black like the cuts on my arms, where the smoke had tattooed the lacerations, all over his face, and I saw in his dark eyes something of the lingering shock that I had seen in my own eyes when I looked at my face on Saturday morning. He had been sitting further forward in the train than me, reading a book. The cuts all over his face were from where the window behind him had exploded. Although I had been two or three feet nearer the bomb, I had fewer glass lacerations, because I was closer to the centre of the carriage where there were no windows, and because I had been protected by the crush of passengers around me. The explosion had damaged Mark's eardrums; a keen diver, he was concerned about whether he would be able to equalise the air pressure next time he dived. He had a dive holiday planned. I commiserated; I hadn't thought about that as a consequence of the explosion, not being able to swim underwater.

J and I poured wine, and we four sat in the scented garden and talked and listened with the instant confidence of shared experience. Asking each other if we remembered this face, that voice, this cry, that sound.

'Did you know it was a bomb? Did you think we were going to suffocate in a fire?'

'Yes, not at first, but later.'

'Did you think we were going to die?'

'Yes. Sometimes. Did you?'

'Yes. At first. Until I heard your voice.'

Mark told me of how he had fixed his mind on his wife Sarah, how he had been so sorry that he was never going to see her again. Neither he nor I had cried since the bomb. Both of us spoke of the flashes of shocked memory, the guilt, and the elation, the desperate trying to make sense of the senseless. The incomprehensible fact that we were both still here. Sarah and J talked too, of the worry and fear, the relief and anxiety, the happiness held to the heart, despite the realisation of the damage done to other homes, other families, as the missing never came home.

I told Mark of how his determination to get back on the tube and face his fears had inspired me to get back to work today. He confided how afraid he had been when travelling, of how he like so many other commuters now dreaded the sudden hiss of brakes, the slowing down in a tunnel, the lack of air in a crowded carriage with no communication from the driver about why the train had stopped between stations. I thought of the journey to work I had to make tomorrow, without J at my side, and how frightened I felt at the thought. J told Mark of how afraid he had felt that morning.

I looked around the table at the four of us and I said I was determined to look into the faces of my fellow travellers tomorrow. Something tube passengers never do. As we left King's Cross station, I would be thinking, like everyone else, of a bang, smoke, screams…

And of whether the face opposite me would be the face that looked into my eyes and held my hand if the unimaginable happened again. Of whether the stranger on the train would be the guide in the panic and the voice in the dark. If these bombs make us realise that we are all fellow travellers, that we all need each other, that we can rely on each other, I said, then something good will come out of this.

We all hugged our goodbyes in the moonlit garden. I wanted to listen to music afterwards, but I could not. I could feel the tears there, ready to fall, but they still would not come. I lit a candle instead, for those who had not come home. I was so glad to have spoken to someone else who had been there. It had helped, more than I knew how to say. I could not sleep that night. I lay awake until four in the morning, eyes wide, thinking, of all the people who had been on the train.

The next day, getting into work left me shattered. My hands shook until lunchtime, which made it hard to use the computer. Twice I had to hide in the loo and have a quick weep. It was the music on the office stereo that I could not bear; any sad song set me off.

At lunchtime I checked on urban75; there was another message from another survivor, called Leo, who had stood opposite me when he boarded at King's Cross. He had read my urban75 account, and Mark's response on the website, and told me he was so happy to have found someone else who was there. I called Mark, and we both emailed him at once. He described what he had been wearing, a stripy jumper, and then I remembered seeing him at Russell Square ticket hall. I had described him in my statement to the police. He, Mark and I all made arrangements to meet up in Trafalgar Square a week after the bombs for the two-minute silence.

My boss came to my desk that afternoon. She gave me the number of a counselling service, said the company would pay for four sessions; it was available to all staff. She said she was incredibly impressed that I had come in, and taken the tube, but she thought that having achieved that hurdle, maybe taking a bit of time off would be a good idea. I was relieved: I had not wanted to ask for time off, as I was new, and didn't want to appear to be feeble, and I had not been badly hurt. But I could see that my work output was rubbish, that I was very, very tired indeed and that I was starting to cry in the office at odd times, which was not great for my team, who didn't know what to do to help me. I headed back home in a cab, paid for by one of the senior directors, who had seen me leaving the office, squeezed my shoulder, passed me his silk handkerchief when the tears started at his kind gesture, and told me I should be proud of myself, and for God's sake, now go home and try to sleep.

I got out of the taxi a few hundred yards from my house, in order to visit the local shop. The Turkish shopkeeper, whom I knew quite well, told me how sorry he was about it all. 'These bad people, they are not Muslims, you know?' I remarked that I had noticed that the local mosque was raising money for the injured; there was a banner outside asking for donations and expressing sympathy for the victims of the bombs. Yesterday there had been a Get Well Soon card through the letterbox from Mohammed the office manager of the local mini-cab firm J and I had used for years, signed by some of the drivers whom we knew. So word had got out locally then. Jane or J must have mentioned it. I was deeply touched and also uncomfortable. I wanted to say *I do not hate Muslims. Please don't think I hate your religion because of this.* But I did not know how to say it, so I smiled and thanked the shopkeeper instead, asked if he knew anyone else who had been caught up in it all. 'Only you,' he said. 'And I am glad you are okay, you are very lucky, maybe God helped you, eh?' I said I was lucky, very lucky indeed.

Then he told me that the bombers' names had been identified: they were British. And they had been suicide bombers. As he said it, he watched my face. I looked down, because I did not know what to say. Then I met his eyes again.

'You're right. They are not Muslims. They are criminals,' I said, flatly.

'They are stupid fools,' said the shopkeeper. 'They have made it bad for all of us, people are afraid.'

'I know,' I said. 'I know. But I think we will all be okay. We have had terrorism in London before, and we managed.'

'In Turkey too,' said the shopkeeper.

'Well, I'm going back to Turkey for my holidays,' I said. 'And if I meet any terrorists I will tell them to piss off. Anyway, at least now we know I am quite difficult for terrorists to kill.'

'Yeah, tell them to piss off from me too,' he said, and we both laughed, but it wasn't that funny and we both knew it.

Walking home from the shop, I felt nothing but the same numb, exhausted sadness. I had not watched the news today; I had not been able to face it before getting on the train to work. I had not expected to find out such news in a shop; the shopkeeper and I didn't normally chat about religion or politics. The weather, the latest local shooting or stabbing in Hackney, and Arsenal's new stadium being built down the road was our usual subject of conversation.

In a strange way I was not surprised to hear that the bombers were young British men. That they had died, well, all I could feel now was that I was glad they were dead. Now I would not have to be angry with them: they no longer existed.

When I had let myself in, made tea and turned on the twenty-four-hour news channel I heard the presenter describing another horrific truck bomb attack in Iraq, which had killed many people including lots of small children. They had run towards the truck hoping for sweets when it exploded. In Iraq, I reflected, it was 7th July every single bloody day. Today, tomorrow, there would be more bombs exploding in Iraq and in other countries, and more people would be terrified, injured. Ordinary people would find themselves running away screaming because of politics, because of religion, because of power struggles that they could not influence or change or control. I turned off the TV; the news was too unbearable to listen to at that moment.

I went to water the parched tomato plants in my garden instead. The BBC team had sent three texts wanting my reaction on the news that the bombers were Brits. In a short while I would need to send over a reaction piece for the BBC website. But for now, I just needed to shut down for half an hour, watch the water splashing onto the warm earth, breathe in the scent of green tomato leaves and geraniums and unhook my racing mind, let it drift and become blank, a leaf on a tree turning in the breeze, absorbing the sunlight, and think of nothing, not writing, not bombs, not work, not politics – nothing at all.

LATER, THAT AFTERNOON, I WROTE the piece for the BBC, making the point that I knew that the Qur'an, the Torah, the Bible, any sacred text could be interpreted to back up all kinds of personal and political agendas. But I had also been taught that all the major world faiths teach of the sanctity and value of life, of how love is more important than hate. I wrote of how I 'didn't want to meet hate with hate. Hate feeds hate. I'm scared, but I'm not that scared.' I didn't know if it would do any good. I didn't want to write about what I really thought, which was that I was terrified that there would be attacks on Muslims and counter-attacks, riots and violence and paranoia and rage and everything would go to hell in a handcart.

By evening, I felt sick with fatigue and anxiety. I finally managed to get hold of my parents, who had been teaching a painting course in rural Norfolk where there was almost no mobile reception. We had been texting regularly, but we had still not been able to catch up properly because they had course students with them all day and most of the evenings. I did my best to allay their worries and tell them that I was fine. Then Leo, who had been on my carriage, rang up. He had found my account on urban75 and sent me a message earlier; we had exchanged messages and phone numbers. We talked on the phone for a long time, making arrangements at the end of the call to meet in Trafalgar Square the next day for the silence in memory of the victims of the bombs. I was becoming aware of just how bad this was for the other people on the train, and how little help there seemed to be for people. It worried me. I closed my phone and sat down on the sofa, unable to speak, or write, or think, or do anything at all for bone-deep weariness. I felt like I had been slammed into a wall. Speechless, because there was nothing I could say that would make this any better, for me or for anyone else. My words, my lucky charms, my defence against disaster had deserted me.

Jane came round and found me staring into space holding an empty mug, the kettle filled but not switched on and the fridge door open and beeping an alarm. She gave me a brisk hug, took the mug from me and made tea, and then set about cooking sausages. J arrived home, looking pale with tiredness. Jane dished up platefuls of food for us all, while J chatted to her in the kitchen. I continued to slump on the sofa, owl-eyed.

We all sat in the garden, eating the sausages while she and J talked of inconsequential things. I still had nothing to say, so I sat and ate my supper in almost-silence; I managed to thank Jane for her kindness and her practical help, but I could not talk properly. My ears hurt, my eyes hurt, and my heart was sore. After Jane had gone back home, I broke down and cried properly, for the first time. J held me while I shook and sobbed. I wept for the poor people who had been standing behind me who had died and been injured. Deep underground in a narrow, dirty, smoke-choked tunnel, in the dark, I had left them there, screaming and crying, dead or dying and I had not been able to help them. I wept with despairing anger at the men who had done this; how could they hate us so much? How could they think it was glorious or just? I cried because I had been so afraid, and because I had survived, and the other passengers behind me had not. The grief storm left me swollen-faced and whimpering, and feeling that strange guilt again, because I knew I had no right to cry so much for strangers, when I was alive and unhurt. J made me blow my nose into a tissue and wiped my face with a wet flannel, as if I was a child. I got into bed, thinking I would remain awake for hours as I had done the previous night, but I fell asleep almost at once.

CHAPTER EIGHT

The rest of July

THE NEXT DAY WAS THURSDAY 14th July, marking a week since the bombs. I could not bear to watch the news, and see the pictures all over again, but J turned on BBC Radio 4 at 8.50am, the time of the explosions. We listened to the stories of people who had been on the trains, those who had rescued people from the tracks, tended the injured ones brought off the bus, searched for the missing, waited and hoped and then despaired. Both J and I cried silently, sitting next to each other on the sofa, not touching.

J went to work, and I left the flat an hour later, and because I was feeling too scared to use the tube, I got a cab to Trafalgar Square where I met Mark and Sarah and Leo, the man in the stripy jumper whom I had spoken to for an hour the night before. Then I had a call from a colleague, Patrick, who had been on another carriage of the train, and who worked upstairs in the same company as me. He had been trapped on the last carriage for forty minutes, breathing smoke with people who thought they were going to die in a fire. He was on his way to join us. We all waited together for the two-minute silence in the Square, underneath the statue of George IV on horseback. Cars stopped, tourists stood with their heads bowed, pigeons hopped at our feet. The Mayor of London had asked people to come out of their offices and stand in the streets to show their solidarity against those who sought to frighten us from living and working and travelling in public for fear of being murdered by a bomb, and all over the UK, people did. Even the Queen was filmed standing with her head bowed outside Buckingham Palace.

After the Silence, which was at noon, we went to the pub and had coffee. Patrick went off back to work, Mark and Sarah to lay flowers at King's Cross, Leo to meet friends. We arranged to meet up later for the Vigil in the evening. I went back out into the Square to buy a sandwich for lunch. My phone rang.

'Hello, is that Rachel? This is Fergal Keane from the BBC. I hope me ringing you up is okay, I got your number off Gary whom you've been writing that amazing diary for. I wanted to interview you, for the *Six O'Clock News*, is that all right, would you mind?'

I didn't mind, as long as I could be just 'Rachel', no surname, and not identified as the author of the BBC bomb diaries. I could see how fixated the media were getting with '7/7 victims' and I didn't want them coming to my flat and wanting to talk to me. But Fergal was a journalist and writer I had long admired for his coverage of the Rwandan genocide and the South African Truth and Reconciliation Commission. I knew he would be good to talk to, and it was an honour to be asked to say something.

'Where?' I asked. There were crews of reporters everywhere still, in Trafalgar Square.

'Not where you are, you'll be eaten alive.' He told me the name of a hotel near Hyde Park, and told me to get in a cab.

Fergal met me in the lobby, with a warm handshake. The cameraman, Fred, was stuck in traffic, he told me, so we had a mineral water and talked for forty minutes. Fergal told me that everyone at the BBC was 'gripped' by the diary, and said that it was 'extraordinary'. I was flustered and somewhat overcome. He said I was brave, that nothing like that had ever happened to him, which considering that he was a war correspondent, I thought was bizarre. We talked about how the bombs had made Fergal feel, remembering a previous IRA bomb attack outside the BBC building. Fergal was angry at the news of the 7th July attacks. 'It was so brutal, so *uncivilised*,' he said, looking into the distance. He told me of a poem that he loved by Irish poet Mark Longley, called 'All of These People'.

'*Who was it who suggested that the opposite of war/is not so much peace as civilisation? He knew/Our assassinated Catholic greengrocer who died/At Christmas, in the arms of our Methodist minister (...) What can bring peace to people who are not civilised?*'

From 'All of these People' from *The Weather in Japan*
by Michael Longley, published by Jonathan Cape.
(Reprinted with permission of The Random House Group Ltd.)

As Fergal quoted the lines he had tears in his eyes.
He had used a line from the poem as the title of his book about

his growing up and his father, and how he became a writer and went to Africa to work in Rwanda as the country began to tear itself apart in bloody civil war. I talked a little of how I loved London, the mixed-up-ness of it, people speaking languages from all over the world, working, travelling, socialising side by side. How I was afraid that we would become suspicious of each other, how that would be a tragedy.

Fergal listened, and then he told me that I was a writer, and that being a writer was what I was supposed to do. I tried to stop him and explain that I worked in advertising. 'It's the other side, the dark side, Fergal, editorial people *despise* advertising people, sales people.' I told Fergal that I had shocked myself by the words that had poured out of me after the bomb and that they had written themselves. I did not know why this writing had suddenly happened, and I did not know if I would be able to keep doing it once my life returned to normal. Fergal was insistent: no, *you are a writer, and you must write every day*. And you must keep in touch with me; I will be watching.

Fred the cameraman arrived then, sparing me from rambling my thanks at this amazing display of faith in me by a respected author, and we went to the park to record the interview, the conversation turning, as we walked, to the less embarrassing subject of Bob Dylan. We did the interview with me sitting on the grass of the park. Afterwards I had my first introduction to the 'walking towards the camera' shot, the opening image for filmed interviews that 'sets the scene'. Fergal told me to start walking, and then laughed as I wandered off into the distance, heading completely the wrong way into the park instead of towards the camera. On my next attempt I was trying so hard not to look at the camera that I nearly walked into a tree and then fell over a small dog. Clearly I was not cut out for a media career. Finally I did it right, and we finished. Fergal and Fred dropped me off in town, and Fergal gave me a souvenir; his Nelson Mandela baseball cap. 'Keep writing,' he said, as I got out of the car. 'Remember, you have to. I will be checking.'

I missed seeing Fergal's 6.00pm *BBC News* report. Instead, I headed back into central London, thinking on his words, to join my friends and my new companions, who had been on the train, at the Vigil in Trafalgar Square. The low evening sunlight shone in our eyes as we stood together, part of a huge crowd that had gathered. We listened to speeches and poems from the Mayor of London, politicians, trade union representatives, religious leaders, TV personalities, and most movingly, the driver of the Edgware Road bombed train. We were told in speech after speech how we are united, unbeatable if we stand together, how 'London will rise'. We were urged to show tolerance, strength, to love and respect each other. Many people were in tears. Sir Trevor McDonald read a Maya Angelou poem in his deep, dignified voice. Richard and Judy Finnegan came on, and were met with cheers and whoops, then some young musicians rapped, with more enthusiasm than skill, and the crowd started to drift away.

As I listened, I thought of how the week had started. How I had been just one of a crowd of Londoners, all hurrying to work, then standing shoulder to shoulder in a crowded carriage, and seconds later, an act of murderous barbarity. Yet almost immediately, even in the choking darkness, in the almost-animal panic, we had remembered our humanity, that we were human beings. We had stood up and comforted each other; we had held hands and led and carried each other to safety. The selfish need to claw and fight for survival, to stampede and try to free ourselves at all cost had not won; instead, the learned behaviour of city dwellers, who must live in close proximity with strangers had taken over.

And I thought of how that had been the message of the week for me: how we are *civilised*, from the Latin word for town-dwellers. We live closely and socially together in crowded cities. We do not always agree with our neighbours; often we do not even talk to each other or look each other in the face. Londoners are often accused of haughtiness and coolness but this week we had felt what it was like to come together as a city. Now we would need to remember what this sense of unity felt like, in the difficult weeks and months ahead. I signed off the BBC journal later that evening, with my thanks and my wishes that we could all carry on our daily lives with calmness and hope. 'Crowded together, shoulder to shoulder,' I wrote, 'I wouldn't have it any other way.'

The comments that began to flood into the BBC as a response to the diary were astonishing. More survivors of the train began to get in touch, partners and friends and colleagues of the survivors said they felt they could understand something of what had happened to people who were caught up in the events. People from all over the world sent their best wishes; many of them had been through devastating events themselves. Many people made their way to the urban75 website and 500 new posters registered in a month, some sending private messages to me via the site. By the next week, ten people from the train had got in touch and I was in email and phone contact with them all.

Media requests also began to pour in, and journalists began to call me and to call the *BBC Online* team who had run my bomb diaries to ask for photographs and interviews. I was wary. I wanted to stay anonymous and the point of the diary was that it could be anyone's story, not Rachel North's story. My phone kept ringing with calls from journalists. I turned down all the requests with as much politeness as I could muster but it was starting to get a bit much. When a nervous-sounding young man from a Sunday newspaper phoned up when I was right in the middle of cooking dinner I let my feelings get the better of me. He asked if I would like to be made-up and photographed and do 'an upbeat, positive feature with us'.

'Like what?' I asked suspiciously.

He explained, 'Maybe a birthday? Wedding? Pregnancy? A happy occasion, post-bombing?'

I couldn't believe it.

'Perhaps "Bomb Victims: What Are They Wearing This Week?"' I suggested. 'Or "Blast Fashion Tips: Match Your Lipstick to Your Stitches". Or "The King's Cross Diet: I Lost Five Pounds in Three days With Post-Traumatic Shock Disorder".'

'Are you, um, taking the mickey?' he asked, uncertainly. 'It's, um, not a fashion piece…'

'Look,' I said, hastily moving the frying pan of onions before it burned. 'I was writing *anonymously* for the BBC. I posted anonymously on a lefty London community website. I should have thought anyone who has read that would see that I have no interest in appearing in a paper that peddles the sort of tripe that you are suggesting. And what I and the other survivors I've met are trying to do is get on with our lives. Not wheel out made-up feel-good women's magazine bollocks to make Tory housewives in Cheshire feel good…'

'We're not as bad as you think,' he said. 'We'd take a different tack…'

'I wouldn't', I said, getting into my stride, 'wipe my arse on your paper if terrorists had blown up every bog roll in London.'

'Hmm, well, in that case, I wish you well', said the young man, 'and I hope that you, um, feel better soon…'

'Oh I do,' I said. 'I feel much better.' He said goodbye and we hung up and I cackled to myself. One–nil. Maybe.

But I could also see that the story seemed to have taken on a life of its own, and somehow it was helping people to understand what had happened. The bombs had mostly exploded where nobody could see them, underground; hundreds of thousands of people used the tube and had read my words and had written to say that they had imagined my experience as their own nightmare. Fifty-two innocent people, and the four bombers were dead; over seven hundred people were injured, many more were very frightened. Muslims in the UK began to say on the news that they feared a backlash, and attacks against people and mosques were reported. Despite my trepidation about the approaches of journalists, I remained hugely impressed with the BBC, so I agreed to do a short interview with the *BBC World Service*, which I knew had an audience of millions of Muslims. I wanted to let people know that I was not angry at Islam, that I knew these attacks were not Islamic. Maybe it would help.

I also agreed to read extracts of my diary for BBC Radio 4's

Broadcasting House, a news and current affairs programme
that my mother and J's mother were fans of. Mixed in with
my words in the report was an interview with a brave Iraqi
doctor whose words reminded me of Fergal Keane's poem.
He said, passionately, 'We are a *civilised* people.' I listened
to him describing how he treated the victims of bombs and
beatings, every day, men, women, little children and I thought
– if he can cling to that hope, that people are civilised, then so
can I damn it. So can we.

THE SUN BEAT DOWN OVER the weekend and I spent
hours reading in the garden with J, mind drifting like a
raft on a still lake. I devoured the new Harry Potter book,
grateful for the distraction into a safer fantasy world where
good prevailed over evil. A woman emailed me to say that she
had read my diary and to tell me that she was worried about
her partner, who had been on the same train as me. She had
found him in a café after a stranger had found him wandering
the streets, in deep shock. He had been 'black with soot, his
clothes torn and splattered with blood, one side of his face
covered in cuts'. His phone had been broken in the blast and,
she wrote, he 'barely knew who he was'. She told me that
he was 'profoundly troubled, preoccupied with the missing,
seemingly convinced that he may recognise them', and how
he was haunted by the conversations he had in the dark with
his fellow passengers. He wanted to talk to someone else
who was there. 'Perhaps a therapeutic pint may be in order?'
she wondered. She went on to say that her father had lost

his colleague to the atrocity and her friend's mother was still missing. 'For some reason this has touched our lives from many sides, yet if I go into work or walk to the shops, it's like it happened in a different country.' It was bleak reading. I felt the weight of feeling responsible for trying to help people, and unsure of what I could possibly do. I sent her my private email and my phone number, told her if she thought I could help, then of course I would do what I could.

That came to eleven people who had got in touch in the last week because of the bomb journal. There were over eight hundred on the train I had been travelling on. Still, it was something, that some of us had found each other and were talking about it. At the moment, though, everyone was talking to me on an individual basis. I thought the sooner we could all get together and go for a drink as a group, the better. I was worried. I wasn't sure if I could cope on my own with being the person people come to for help. I didn't know what I was doing. I wasn't trained for this. But at the same time, I wanted to help. Perhaps it was guilt because I could not help people on the day. Maybe it was because I had the heads-up on PTSD already because of the rape: most people didn't know what it was. I didn't want people to be left in the dark and not know what to do about the bad dreams, the shock, the startle reactions, and the isolation that trauma can bring in its wake. In any event, I was going to try to do what I could, even if I was anxious about it all. Talking to people, writing back to their emails, it was a small thing to do. I was lucky to be able to do it. It was just a bit overwhelming at times. But that was probably because I wasn't sleeping well.

On Monday 18th July I was back at work, and I still could

not get away from the subject of the bombs. Patrick, the young man from my office who had been travelling further back on the same train, wanted to talk about it. He was clearly still in shock, afraid to ask for time off, afraid of being seen as weak. He would only talk about how he felt to me 'because you were there, Rachel'. He wouldn't even talk to his mum. I finally persuaded him to see his GP and take some time off. 'For starters, Patrick, if you are going to claim for compensation from the Criminal Injuries fund because of your ears being hurt, you need to let them know that you were there, that you were affected.'

I still couldn't sleep, despite paying for a back massage. J was working late on a deal that was likely to have him doing sixteen-hour days all week, and I missed him. I would sit on the sofa, then jump up and pace about the house, unable to keep still. I couldn't concentrate on reading books or watching television, and when friends or family phoned I had little to say; I didn't want to talk about the bombs any more, but I could think of little else. Family and friends did not want to tell me about their problems because of what had happened to me. So there was a distance between us. I was afraid to go to sleep on my own because of the nightmares that came every night, so I mostly sat in the bath, thinking, until the water went cold and my fingertips were raisined.

On Tuesday I finally managed to get hold of Ian, one of my best friends, whose mother had died a week before of cancer. Though we had been sending text messages to each other, we had not been able to talk on the phone. While I had been consumed with the fall-out after the bomb, and trying to manage work, and help the other passengers who had got in

137

touch, Ian had been caught up in his own private grief. I was angry with myself that I had let the terrorist attack get in the way of me being there when he needed his friends.

On Wednesday 20th July I had my stitches taken out. The cut was healing well, it would leave a bumpy, jagged scar, but once again I had been lucky. The shard of metal had been embedded deep in my wrist bone, like an arrow sticking in a target board. If it had caught the soft underside of my wrist as I raised my arms in a protective reflex to cover my head and ears, it would have sliced deep into my artery. I wondered where the metal had come from; whether the bomb had been a nail bomb. The news still would not give details.

After visiting the doctor I caught a late-morning almost-empty Victoria line to work. Once again, I got into the first carriage. I realised that I was checking the surroundings out like an SAS officer: *Who is on the tube? Description? Demeanour?* I sat by the door (*easier exit*), then moved a place (*because mustn't be close to the glass partition, might get hit by flying glass*). As if it made any difference, as if by moving about I could stop myself from getting blown up if anyone wanted to get on the train with another rucksack full of explosives. I was playing games with myself to feel safer, but I was not safe.

I got off at Warren Street, walked the last fifteen minutes to the office with my lips pressed together, striding, hair flying like a Valkyrie, on a mission to punch dozy tourists with backpacks out of the way. Work was still weird; I would try to concentrate on a spreadsheet and the figures would blur in front of my eyes. Colleagues kept coming over and saying that they were glad to see me, and then looking embarrassed and saying, 'you must be fed up with people saying that'. I replied each time, absolutely truthfully, that I was very grateful for people's good wishes, it had made a real difference. I wanted to hug them. But you can't do that sort of thing in an open plan office with people you have only known for seven weeks.

After work, I met my friend Dave for a pint. His friend Liz was the thirty-ninth victim to be identified as having died on 7th July; she had been travelling in my carriage. She had worked as a manager in the neuroradiology department of University College Hospital, where I and many others had been treated on 7th July. I had been meant to join Dave and Liz and her boyfriend Rob on a walk earlier in the year; Dave had invited me along but I had pulled out at the last minute. I kept thinking, what if I had gone on the walk? I might have recognised Liz on the train, called her over to chat with me in the front of the train a few yards from where she stood, and she might not have died. More guilt. Dave and I talked about taking sides. Love or hate. Civilisation or barbarism. Nihilism or hope. We drank to Liz and Rob, and we tried not to cry.

Afterwards, I went to King's Cross station, to the make-shift memorial garden that had sprung up outside the station entrance, where people had been leaving flowers. The flowers were dying now. There were many messages, of outrage and hope and grief, from all over the world: all of the world is in London. I put some blue cornflowers there and left a message.

To my fellow passengers. I got off the train. I am so sorry that I had to leave you there. When we all got on that train we did not know that for some of us it would be our last journey and that some of us would not come home. We did not finish our journey together but I carry you in my heart now and so do millions of other people. To all that loved you, knew you, worked with you, miss you, my thoughts are with you. At the end of the journey we are all fellow passengers, and we can all hold hands in the dark,

Rachel

Then I sat in a bar with J, and I drank again to the dead and the injured, as tears dripped silently off my nose. And we got a cab home.

THE NEXT DAY, THURSDAY 21ST July, J and I both overslept, and we caught a cab into work together. As we went past University College Hospital I had an unexpected, overwhelming reaction of utter horror. The reaction I should have had, but didn't have when I went there in a taxi after the bomb at exactly the same time in the morning a fortnight before. Covered in soot and blood with blasted hair and a bleeding wrist. I had forgotten that it was a Thursday morning and two weeks exactly since the bombs had gone off, but my body had remembered. I got out of the cab in Gower Street, feeling physically sick with fear. My stomach was cold and cramping, as if I had eaten ice cubes. My breath came in short gasps. My lips were numb and I could feel my heart banging in my chest. The street was shimmering and moving as if I was viewing it underwater. I did not recognise that I was having a panic attack at first. Then I remembered what to do: *Breathe. Keep breathing. Don't double over, stand up, feel your feet on*

the ground; this is not real, it is just your body remembering, there are no bombs today, you are safe.

Ten minutes later I had composed myself enough to walk into the office, and I headed for the loo because my guts were twisted with pain. I threw up, carefully, holding back my hair, and splashed my face, powdered my nose and wiped off the panda-blotches of mascara. I went straight to my boss and apologised for being late in; she was gentle with me, which nearly set me off again. I didn't explain what had happened. I had no sane-sounding explanation to give her for why passing an A&E department in a taxi should make me feel violently ill.

By lunchtime I was shaking with tiredness again, trying to catch up with work at my computer station. The rest of the office headed out to get something to eat for lunch, but I wasn't hungry. When they had gone, I rested my pounding head on my hands briefly. My boss came up silently behind me and tapped me on the shoulder.

'How's it going?'

I jumped up, pushing my hair back. 'Oh fine. Sorry, just resting my eyes for a moment.'

She looked at me. 'Whatever it is you're working on, it can wait. Go home. You can ring Jenna or Warren later if you need someone to do your stuff. You look shattered.'

I set off for Warren Street on the Victoria line, feeling an unprofessional failure. I couldn't believe it was still affecting me so much. A few hundred yards from the tube station, I decided on an impulse to turn back; the pain in my head was starting to gather over my right eye, an ominous warning of an approaching migraine, probably brought on by my clenching my jaw all morning and by being dehydrated. I walked instead to Neal's Yard back-rub centre, a walk-in massage place where therapists sit you on a treatment chair and work on your back through your clothes, for ten or twenty minutes to uncrunch and unwind you. From experience, someone working on the knotted muscles in my back and neck could fend off a headache more quickly than taking codeine tablets. As the massage therapist started to work on my muscles, my eyes began to water again, but nobody noticed, and the tension and pain began to leave my head as her gentle hands kneaded my neck.

By the time twenty minutes had passed I felt much better. I decided to go back to work and see if I could use my new-found energy to shift some of the backlog of emails that had developed while I was off. When I got in, there was a strange sense of tension in the office and no music was playing. Only a few people were sitting at their desks, the rest of them were standing round a TV screen, which was tuned to *BBC News 24* and showing breaking news. People turned to me as I came closer to see what was happening, their faces anxious. Jenna caught hold of my arm. 'Rach, sit down. There's been another one.'

'*What?*'

'Nobody was killed…'

I went straight to the TV to find out what the news reader was saying, conscious that Jenna at my side was signalling to my boss to come over. I listened to the news and found out what had happened.

Just after I had turned away from Warren Street tube station and started heading back to the massage shop, four more bombs had been detonated. One at Warren Street, two more at two other tube stations and one on a bus at Bethnal Green. The reports said that the Warren Street bomber had fled towards University College Hospital. The bombs had caused small explosions, probably the detonators, but it seemed that the main charge had not gone off, instead a strange smell was reported and a hissing, fizzing substance leaking out of the back packs that the bombers had carried.

It was too much, and I was not able to stop myself sitting down at my desk and bursting into tears. As I shook, Jenna and my colleagues clustered about me and patted me; many of them looked white with shock as well. There were several sticky post-it notes on my computer screen: Patrick, the colleague from the bombed train, had been trying to get hold of me. I called him back quickly.

'Rach, I don't like this. At all. How are you feeling? Are you okay, mate?'

'I don't like it either. I'm okay, but I'm a bit shocked. I feel sick…'

'Have you got someone with you?'

'Yeah. Have you?'

'Yeah. I feel sick as well. *Bastards.*'

'Okay, look, stay with people, try and stay cool. I'll be up in a minute.' As I spoke, my mobile phone began to fill up with text messages from the other King's Cross survivors who had emailed and got in touch via urban75 and the BBC since the bomb. I sent round a quick email, texted everyone back: they were all okay. We made tentative arrangements to meet in a week's time if the bombers struck again next Thursday. I pointed out in the email that the likelihood of us all being bombed again, together, was 'bloody slim. We've a better chance of winning the lottery.'

'We should probably start a syndicate then, my luck is bloody weird at the moment,' someone emailed back.

I found Patrick upstairs, pale and set-faced, sitting at his desk and shaking, like I had been, with his colleagues standing round him protectively. I gave him a hug. We made a command decision to leg it; I was sick of trying to be stoical and stiff-upper-lipped in the face of more bombing attempts. I felt like screaming. Patrick called for a taxi while I did a quick work handover with my team, writing some quick notes for Jenna and Warren, and then Patrick and I both left the office in a rush. I felt the adrenalin thundering through me again. I was sweating with anxiety, and this time, anger was rising, rising like a wave. I held my fists in my lap so Patrick wouldn't see how furious and trembling I was, and dug my nails into my palms.

'Can you drive any faster?' Patrick asked the cabbie. 'I just want to get out of the West End.'

'Everyone's legging it home today, aren't they?' he said.

'Yep,' I replied. 'I can kind of understand why they might want to.'

Once I had got Patrick safely to Finsbury Park station, I went home, and hit the whisky. Called J, told him that I loved him. I couldn't say it enough at the moment. 'Can you come home, sweetheart?'

'No. There's this bloody deal to finish. And there's a helicopter hovering over Ludgate Hill. I think the office might be sealed anyway.'

'For Christ's sake. This is ridiculous.'

'I know. But I have to stay and get this done. It'll be another late one, I'm afraid. I'm sorry, honey. Call Jane. She might come over for tea or something.'

I called Jane, she said she'd be over in an hour. I picked up the cat, and stroked her soft tabby fur. She dug her claws into me and struggled; I was holding her too tight. I started to write again on my new blog, 'Rachel from North London', where I was continuing my diary after the BBC bomb journal had finished. I didn't know what else to do, or if anyone would ever read it. But at least writing calmed me down. Outside the flat I could hear sirens; they made me jump every time. Jane came round and I made us some supper and we drank a lot of cups of tea. I managed to make her laugh as we talked about the inept bombers, running away, trailing wires. I made joke after joke, becoming almost hysterical with laughter. She went back to her own flat after a few hours, and I waited up until 3.00am for J, but he did not come home. I fell asleep in my clothes on the sofa, holding a cushion. I woke in a panic at 6.45am to find that he had still not returned.

J finally got back at 7.45am, looking drained. I embraced him, my head aching. The failed bombers did not seem so funny today. I recognised yesterday's euphoria as a re-run of the same survivor reaction. Numbness–euphoria–anger–anxiety–euphoria–numbness, the 7th July reactions moving through me again and again like the ripples from a rock heaved into a still pond. Repeat to fade.

J and I sat watching the breakfast news, which was all about the attempted bombings. We started making dark predictions about when the next one would happen. I guessed the eighth of the eighth for the next big attack. The Jubilee, Northern,

Central and Bakerloo lines still had not been bombed. Stratford and Euston station were my predictions. But with two attacks in two weeks, all bets were off. The landscape of London felt subtly changed by fear: a toxic, invisible gas. It was frightening to think of how this sick sense of foreboding and suspicion could change London, change how it felt to live in this busy, tolerant city.

I texted work to explain that I needed to take the morning off as holiday, because I had not slept and felt unwell, and they said, chill, take it as sick leave and come in on Monday. J and I managed to get some sleep for a few hours. Looking at myself in the mirror when I got up I looked noticeably older, with dark rings under my eyes and a pale puffy face. J called sleepily from the bedroom.

'What time is it?'

'It's lunchtime. Stay in bed.'

'No, I have to go back to work.'

'For Christ's sake, J, you've just worked twenty-four hours straight. You've had three hours sleep; don't be mad. You're killing yourself.'

'The deal needs to be done today. I'm going in.'

'*I don't want you to.* Please. This is insane. *Look at the bloody news.*'

'I can't help it. I have to. It's my job. *Don't make this any worse than it is.*'

I gave up and made him a cup of tea. When he had gone – taking the tube – I sat on the sofa, with the newspaper J had brought back that morning, reading the pages comparing the details of the two bomb attacks – the 7th July and the 21st July. Afterwards I sat still for a long time with my head in my hands – and wondered what the hell to do, and how we were all going to get through this madness. My parents called and said they were going to drive up from Norfolk to see me tomorrow. I was glad that they were coming, even gladder that they weren't going to come on the overground or underground trains. I turned off the news, and curled myself into a ball on the sofa, tried to sleep again, but sleep would not come, so I went to the computer and wrote about how I was feeling instead. It helped. A bit. At least it stopped me getting drunk and screaming at things and frightening the cat and the neighbours.

When I turned on the news again later, I found out that the police had shot dead a suspected suicide bomber that morning on the tube, at Stockwell, on the Northern line. The man had been shot several times in the head, at point blank range. This was new and horrifying territory.

It got worse. The man was later found to be an innocent electrician from Brazil, Jean Charles de Menezes. And on Saturday, another suicide bomb exploded in Egypt, killing eighty-three people, holidaymakers, divers, tourist industry workers. My parents arrived and we sat in the garden and talked and talked; later we went to a local Turkish restaurant and feasted on fire-grilled lamb. I wrote on my blog of how I knew love could defeat fear, how fear was an injury that I knew would fade in time, that despite all these bombs and deaths I still believed that people were good – as I had seen on 7th July, when strangers grabbed each others' hands in the dark and helped each other avoid panic, how passers-by had rushed to help. Mostly I believed what I was saying.

I went back to work and got straight into a big pitch,

working long hours and struggling because the lack of sleep made my thinking muddled at times. The adrenalin continued to keep me going, but my eyes were raw and itchy and my back was solid with stress. More emails arrived from fellow-survivors, telling me terrible things. I pulled myself together and organised a meet-up at an Islington pub at the end of the month for the people from the train who had got in touch with me.

We met on a warm Thursday night, in the back of The Bull, a large cheerful Islington pub on Upper Street. I had asked the staff to find us a place where we could sit and where the music could be kept low, as I knew many people had hearing problems after the explosion had damaged their ears. We were nervous at first, strangers from the train who would never normally talk to each other, only push through the doors each morning looking for a seat or a place to stand before burying our noses in a newspaper or book. How many of us had travelled the same route day after day, sitting or standing in the same place, never noticing the other passengers until that moment when the lights had gone out and the screaming began? Yet by the end of the evening, we were talking and laughing like old friends. The bonds of shared experience, the relief of finding others whose story was the same – and the rounds of drinks we bought each other carried us on a surge of giddy gratitude and camaraderie. The evening went on until 11.30, and we were the last to leave the pub. 'I am so bloody glad that I have found you all,' was heard again and again. 'We need to keep in touch, we have to do this again,' someone said, and there were nods of agreement.

Jane, who worked in web advertising, volunteered to set up

a group email messaging system so we could keep in contact. 'Oh, brilliant idea.' 'We need a name,' someone else said. I looked at everyone's animated faces. We already felt like a team, united against the horrors of the darkness.

'King's Cross United,' I said, immediately. 'That's who we are. What do you think?' And everyone agreed, and that was how we started, the little group of shaken passengers in a pub, that went on to become a self-help group over a hundred strong.

There were more emails and phone calls from journalists, asking for interviews, all of which I declined. Someone accused me via a blog comment of 'loving all this attention', and of being 'self-indulgent', and I briefly felt almost violent towards them. *Do you think I want this life? Why don't you try and live through this and see if you do any better? I'm not getting paid for this, you stupid, stupid bastard. This feels like a full-time job, one I never bloody asked for. I don't know why I am doing this, or feeling this, or what the hell is wrong with you, or what the hell is wrong with me. But leave me out of this attack, please, you don't know me. You don't have any damn idea.*

I stopped writing, stopped doing anything apart from work on the pitch. I didn't want to talk about the bombs to anyone any more, but still people called and emailed wanting to tell their stories, wanting my story, wanting other people's stories, which I would not tell. I was angry and sorry for myself, wretchedly guilty for feeling sorry for myself, and pretty much at the end of my rope. The month of July, which had begun so sweet and hopeful, ended. And for the most part, all I could feel was a sickening, ever-present fear, and a deadening despair.

CHAPTER NINE

Are you seeing someone?

THERAPY. COUNSELLING. IT WAS A mantra, recommended by everyone. 'Are you seeing someone?' It was a rhetorical question; counselling was the panacea, the magic bullet everyone believed in. I was not sure if it would work for me. I felt guilty about explaining this, so I usually nodded, and said yes, giving people permission not to worry about me.

I had seen someone; four sessions had been paid for by work; I saw them no longer. In the first few weeks after the bomb in July, I had gone to an office in Holborn where I had sat opposite a man who reminded me of Tim Robbins in the film *The Shawshank Redemption*, both in his owl-glasses appearance and in his quiet strength. He explained to me that he specialised in dealing with clients who had undergone severe trauma. I felt relieved. He was not what I called the 'whale-song and inner child brigade'. I did not think at the time that I could cope with anyone offering me sympathy or saying, 'Oh my dear, how terrible'. I did not want mothering, or to have my vulnerability acknowledged, I was far too afraid of that edifice falling and of me disintegrating in a whimpering snot-storm of babyish tears. What I wanted was a cool assessment of whether I was likely to cope, over the weeks and months ahead, and whether I was normal.

I sat opposite the therapist, reeking of the three cigarettes I had smoked in quick succession while hurrying to his office from my own.

'I've had PTSD before', I said, my voice carefully flat, 'and I know from my studying the subject that a second traumatic experience can cause compound PTSD, more problems. I can't afford that to happen. I need to know the prognosis, how I present.' I might as well have been talking to someone who was surveying my house for flood damage, or a mechanic looking at a pranged car. Only my hands, twisting on my lap, and my muscle jumping as I chewed my cheek gave the game away.

'Tell me what happened to you,' he said, quietly.

I told him, in a flat voice entirely devoid of emotion, of almost all that I had seen and felt and heard at the time on 7th July. 'I should explain', I said, after I had finished, 'that I don't feel anything as I am telling you this. I might as well be reading the news.'

'Does it feel real?' he asked.

'Not when I tell you about it. Is that – normal?'

'That's normal,' he said.

I felt relief. 'You see', I went on, in a rush, 'I am not sure if talking, counselling will work on me. I've had it before.'

'What was that about?' he asked me.

I went on to explain a little of my back-story. In 1998, I had decided to start seeing a counsellor about the depression that had begun to dog me, mainly caused, I thought, by my dissatisfaction with my disjointed double life. I had been in a five-year relationship with a man who lived in Wales, a man whom I had had a crush on at school. We had grown up in Norfolk, been to the same teenage parties. Then I went to work in a busy advertising sales office in central London and he moved into a falling-down cottage near Mumbles. He was on the dole. He seemed to me to have a life of rural freedom that I missed during the week of financial targets and client meetings and PowerPoint presentations and daily clashes with my annoying boss, as I commuted to my desk, sweating nose pressed to the windows of a crowded tube to work every morning. And so, for five years, I had travelled to his damp and carpetless hovel in the Welsh countryside most weekends to see him and to live what I romantically thought of as my secret life. My weekend lover had a motorcycle, various cars in various stages of disrepair onto which squawking chickens clambered and through which weeds poked, drifting friends who lived mainly by dealing dope, organising raves and parties, spending their lives in a haze of stoned smoke, growing their own vegetables and keeping poultry, trading skills and work in return for food and goods. Their slacker lives revolved around smoking, music and avoiding work and the mainstream. On the train down to meet my boyfriend I would change out of my suit that I wore for my advertising sales job, into dirty combats and clumping boots, changing from city girl into someone who looked like a road protester.

I thought I loved him, but was constantly gnawed by not

fitting into either world, my hectic London life of money and financial targets, networking with colleagues and wine after work, wearing the right shoes and hair and face and attitude, or his world of stoned nonconformity and shivering poverty. Sometimes he was casually unfaithful to me, other times he melted me by spending the day cleaning his filthy cottage and making cheese pastries for me in his unspeakable fridgeless kitchen. Occasionally I felt like Maid Marian hurrying from the greedy, jaded, ruthless city to meet her Green Man, her woodland god, his silky muscles hardened by chopping wood for the stove, his frame wiry from lack of food, his eyes dreamy with sweet smoke and tenderness. At other times I wondered what I was doing sitting bored on a damp mat on an earth floor, while some stoned wispy-bearded strangers I didn't know and didn't like banged away on an African drum and shot me occasional pitying glances while they droned on about shamanic mushrooms and Third Eyes.

Now and again my lover would come and visit me in London, hitching up if the motorcycle was broken, but my housemates didn't like it much. They said he smelled. And he did. His motorcycle leathers reeked and there wasn't hot water often in his cottage unless you spent hours chopping wood, so his clothes were not washed too often. You didn't notice in Wales, because of the wood smoke hazing the air, and the lack of central heating. On the 5am train back to London, when I was coming back from visiting him, I would strip off my dirty clothes and shiveringly wash myself in the sink in the grim train toilets, returning fifteen minutes later with my hair in a neat ponytail, in a black trouser suit and boots and a pearl pendant hanging round my neck. Once, the woman commuter who was sitting next to me on the train stopped me as I went to sit back down.

'There was someone else sitting here,' she said, 'a hippie girl.' She wrinkled her nose.

'She's definitely gone,' I said, and sat down, opening my book.

It was an unsatisfactory way to live, and increasingly I wondered who I was and what I was doing with my life. A woman at work in whom I had confided a little suggested I saw her friend, who was training to be a counsellor and would see clients cheaply while she trained. So I went and made an appointment. The 'Transpersonal' counselling and psychotherapy training centre recommended to me was of a somewhat mystical bent, and while I waited, I would browse leaflets offering courses in meditation, archetypes, yoga, the Child Within. This appealed to me at the time. Perhaps this was a way to integrate my dazed weekends and my tendency towards anarchy and hippiedom with my structured weekdays working for Mammon. On a hunch, I signed up for the first-year course. I thought it would be an interesting project and I liked learning new things. And though I wasn't very impressed with the few therapy sessions I had had, perhaps, I reckoned, I could work it out better for myself.

The trainee therapist and I continued to be at odds during our weekly sessions, I often got the impression that she did not like me, and I did not like her. I found her smug and superficially glib, and I knew she found me uncooperative, irritable and uncommitted. I was interested in psychology as a subject, fascinated by it, but the client-therapy relationship with her left me cold. At the time, I thought of a therapist as someone paid to sit and listen to the client talk, and paid to pretend to care. The centre placed a good deal of emphasis on 'person-centred therapy', the idea that the therapist cared for the client and gave of themselves during the relationship of healing. But they went too far; they also talked of 'love'.

Arrogant and headstrong, I saw this as fake. I had friends who I knew would listen to me and impart their wit and wisdom for free, as I would for them, and I had a deep British mistrust of therapy's claims to be 'holding' and 'modelling' the perfect relationship space – the idea that the theatre of the client's desires and dreams and hates and mistrusts could be played out and understood through the spaces between what was said and not said in a room with a stranger paid to listen. Nonetheless I enjoyed the intellectual challenge of the course, and the friends I made there, though some of the more esoteric notions of 'soul' and 'spirituality' and even, once, hilariously, astrology, made me gnash my teeth. I was looking for answers, but intellectual ones, not 'emotional development' or 'personal growth' or 'soul-journeying', which I found slightly embarrassing and un-English. I left the course towards the end of the year, having decided that 'transpersonal therapy' was not for me, either as a career or as a client. The relationship with my woodland drifter ended as soon as J walked into my life and I danced nearer and nearer to him at a party. I fell in love, and the fogs of depression lifted as my feet touched the ground once more.

After the rape in 2002, I had been advised to seek counselling again, and had returned to the Transpersonal Centre to find a counsellor. I saw a gentle Jewish grandmother in Hampstead for a few weeks in August, who took me on as an emergency as therapists were scarce in August, most of them taking that month off. She talked to me like a wise aunt, and midwifed me through the violence of my night-terrors and crucifying flashbacks, helping me find visualisations that made me feel safer, gave me safe refuge in a storm of horror. She could not take me on long term, and so I was passed on to a woman therapist who practised locally, a quiet-spoken, slightly nervous soul whose empathy and desire to help made me wary of burdening her with the extent of my rage. Then finally I saw a Buddhist man, whom I admired greatly but again failed to feel comfortable enough with to tell him the extent of the horror and revulsion I still felt churning inside.

In the end, I walked away from it all. It had helped, some of the time, given me a few practical things I could do to manage the PTSD, some understanding of what was normal, but it was expensive and time consuming and I was always too conscious of holding myself back. There was a voice that I heard throughout every single therapy session I had ever attended, every class in counselling and psychoanalytic theory, every book I read on the subject, every conversation I had. *Self-indulgent. Self-indulgent.*

I explained some of this to the Holborn trauma therapist, and said that I was grateful to him and to my company for paying for the four sessions and that what I wanted was his professional opinion as to whether I was likely to crack up. And some kind of feedback as to how he thought I was coping and what I could do to manage things without letting myself and everybody else down.

'You seem very guarded,' he said. 'You don't seem to think that you deserve therapy, or that you need it.'

'There are people a lot worse off than me,' I said. 'I'm okay, at least I know what PTSD is and what to expect and that I'm not going mad. I'm lucky. I wasn't hurt. I got off the train.'

'Tell me again about how you got off the train,' he said, looking at his notes.

I told him again, in the same polite newsreader voice.

'You seemed to be very calm then, as well,' he said. 'You helped to keep people calm, you helped to get people off the train, you told them it was going to be all right, you even made jokes...'

'Like I said, I felt I was trained for that kind of thing. I was ready,' I said. 'I knew what to do. I just did it. It wasn't as if I was being brave or anything, I just went onto automatic pilot.'

'How could you be ready for that kind of thing?' he asked. 'You were on the way to work, like everybody else. You aren't trained to deal with bombs going off on the train and people dying. Even firemen, police officers, soldiers aren't trained to cope with that happening on the way to work on the tube.'

'I was on the way to work reading about what it was like when everything goes black and there's a huge violent bang on the head and you nearly die,' I pointed out. 'That put me in a different place to everyone else, probably.'

'Then again', he said, 'it could have completely flattened you. You were in a state of horror and shock already when the bomb went off, it could have overwhelmed you and made you give up completely, go to pieces.'

'Well,' I said. 'It didn't. So I was lucky. It made me go very calm and start telling people not to panic.'

'You strike me as having been like an army platoon leader,' he said. 'You helped to take control and evacuate the train. Then you've set up this survivor group, you've reported back from the front line for the BBC, you've been busy keeping up morale. You've been working very hard, haven't you?'

'I don't know.' I said. 'It wasn't enough. I didn't do enough. When I got out of the tunnel, I couldn't do it any more. I had to get away. I went to hospital in a taxi. There were people dying, they were bringing out bodies, there were people injured and I couldn't help them.' I began to shake. 'I've had some first aid training. I couldn't help them. I left them behind.'

I closed my eyes as a wave of revulsion hit me. I was back in the tunnel, the bang, the grinding of brakes, the screams, the falling glass. I bent forward in my chair and covered my face with my hands. The voice started up again. *Self-indulgent, self-indulgent...*

I wondered what I was doing there. I got up, and asked to be excused to get a glass of water and go to the loo. When I got back, I asked him how I was doing.

'We have five minutes left,' he said. 'And this is our last session that your company will pay for. I'd like you to carry on seeing someone.'

'But how am I doing now?' I asked.

'You are presenting the symptoms of severe trauma. Flashbacks, re-experiencing the bomb, hyper-vigilance, disturbed sleep and emotions, intense emotional state, which you are managing to control quite well, but which is clearly causing you to be exhausted from running on adrenalin. You are also suffering from intense survivor guilt, which is not rational, or reasonable under the circumstances, especially considering what you did, but is a symptom of your trauma. It is likely that this trauma has reawakened parts of the earlier trauma, which can sometimes lead to something that we call complex PTSD, so things are challenging for you at the moment. All of this is quite normal, because the bomb happened only a few weeks ago. Your symptoms are not full-blown post-traumatic stress disorder symptoms, because several months have not passed. You are simply, and quite naturally, showing the symptoms of deep trauma and shock, which I would expect, because the event was deeply traumatic and shocking and it happened very recently indeed.'

'Thank you', I said, gratefully, 'for telling me that it is all normal.'

'Entirely normal', he said, 'and as you know, specialist trauma therapy is not necessarily recommended in the first few weeks after a traumatic incident, because the mind and body need time to heal and there is no point saying you have a shock disorder in the first few weeks, because you haven't; you have an entirely natural set of shocked symptoms and reactions which may well go away in time. But, Rachel, you do need to look after yourself more.'

'I am,' I said. 'I have family and friends, and people at work are being great, and I am talking to other survivors...'

'That is not looking after yourself, Rachel,' he said seriously. 'That is looking after them. Ever since that bomb went off', he said, taking off his glasses and wiping them, 'you have been on duty. Trying to keep people calm, keeping up morale, like I said, getting people off that train. And you are still there. You are still in that mode of getting people off that train and trying to look after them. And you are manic.

You are chain smoking, you are shaking, you are drinking too much, you aren't sleeping, you are driving yourself very, very hard indeed. You are looking after other people but you are not looking after yourself, and you are not letting other people look after you, not even me, and you are beating yourself up for not saving everyone on that train and you keep telling me that it was your job to do what you did, even though, Rachel, it wasn't. You were just an ordinary person trying to get to work that morning, and you were not trained and you did what you could and you did a lot. And I am worried about you. So I think you should come back.'

I said I would think about it. I told him that I was grateful that he had seen me, and that he had helped. I said I would be in touch. I could feel my eyes becoming hot with suppressed tears, and my breath becoming shallow.

Inside I felt that he had seen into me and understood what was happening too clearly, and I was afraid. I suddenly couldn't wait to get out of there, the squirming feeling of being over-exposed and pitied and sympathised with was threatening to make me break down. I was too frightened of that happening to stay in the room any longer. I muttered something about going over the time allocated.

He shook my hand. 'Look after yourself, Rachel,' he said, 'and give me a call.'

I shook his hand and bolted out the door and down the stairs. I didn't go back. Writing this now, a year and a half later, I wish that I had.

I CONTINUED TO WRITE THE blog, but I never wrote about my therapy sessions in it: some things were too private to be shared with an internet audience. I did touch on it, though, in an entry I wrote in early October, in which I tried to cheer myself and the blog readers up. More dutiful morale boosting again. That therapist's words had got to me a little bit after all, and I can see now I was defending myself against what they had stirred up in me.

CHAPTER TEN

August 2005 – smoke lingers

I DID NOT FEEL LIKE 'one of the London bombing victims'. I had not died, nor had I been maimed or badly injured. I did not feel like a 'victim'; I hated the word. Nor did I particularly feel like a 'survivor'. It was disconcerting suddenly being referred to as 'Rachel, a bomb survivor' instead of 'Rachel, the vicar's eldest daughter' or 'Rachel, J's girlfriend' or 'Rachel who works on the first floor strategy team' or any of the other things that had previously defined who I was. My BBC diary had now been read by hundreds of thousands of people, and I was nonplussed realising that however many people I knew in my life, or would go on to meet in the future, far more than that would already know about one week in my life. And that would be all they would ever know about me, that story, even if I lived to be a hundred. The BBC diary had been read by people all over the world, it had a far bigger reach and impact than I would ever have, whatever I went on to do in my life. That shattered journey to work, how I felt and how I acted, and afterwards, how I had stumbled away and on through the rest of the week seemed to have taken on 'defining moment of my life' status. I was 'the bomb diary woman'.

I didn't want that. I'd had a life before 7th July, one that now seemed to have disappeared. Before the bomb, I had worked hard at my career, my friendships and relationships. I had achieved some things in my life that I was proud of and I wanted to achieve more things in the future. I had plans, like everyone else. I was a private individual, living a normal life, nobody special. I hadn't chosen to enter a war zone. Being blown up was just something that had happened to me in an instant, one morning on the way to work. But it was all people wanted to talk to me about now. I felt trapped in the role of unwilling extra in a global news story that felt out of control. And although there were hundreds of people who had been directly involved and had far more to say than me, they were not as visible. Because I had written about my day, when I was still in shock, on an internet message board late at night, and then agreed to write some updates, and then kept an online blog, like millions of other people, I had somehow ended up being someone that journalists wanted to talk to. Why? I didn't have any special insight or status. I was trying to remain anonymous, and what was there to say? *I could be anyone, I could be you.* I had no special wisdom. The bombs had affected lots of people. I was just one of many. And lots of people were a lot worse than me. Another reason to feel guilty.

Stories about the bombings continued to dominate the media

and there was no getting away from it. From the moment I woke up and put on the breakfast news, there were frequent references to bombs and terror. The newspapers I read on the way to work, the tubes, the buses, the sirens in the streets, the music I couldn't bear to listen to on the radio, almost everything reminded me of it. It became overwhelming. I stopped feeling like a normal person, stopped connecting with the world outside, all I could think about, dream about was the bombs. All my small hopes and plans and worries were utterly subsumed by this terrible thing that had happened. I would be in the room when people were talking, but I wasn't really present any more; inside I kept going back into the tunnel.

The initial protective shock and euphoria had faded away, and I was sobering up from the impressive cocktail of chemicals my body had generated to cushion me from experiencing too much, too hard, too soon. I was sorry that the protective blanket numbing me from remembering everything in the first few weeks had vanished: without it I felt as raw as a sea creature winkled out of its hard shell. Now that my body chemistry was resetting to normal, the frozen memories I had suppressed began to leak into my consciousness, sometimes all in a jumble together, sometimes piece-by-piece, one sensation, one picture, one recollection at a time. I knew logically, that I had somehow to integrate the experience of the bomb into all the other memories I had before the bomb, make it just one more experience in my life, one day among many; only then could I put it to one side. But it was very hard because I had little control of what was going to crawl out of my subconscious mind and come at me from one moment to the next.

The memories were becoming frighteningly intrusive; they were coming back faster and clearer, more and more frequently, more real than reality at times. I would light a cigarette and not taste it; instead I would taste the black smoke from the tunnel, feel its particular texture in my throat, how my chest and lungs felt sodden and heavy with grit, chemicals, dust, vaporised blood. I would still smoke though; because if I concentrated hard enough, breathing in and out slowly, pressing my feet into the floor to connect with the earth turning slowly underneath me, I could eventually taste the cigarette and reconnect with the world outside my head. When I concentrated on the cigarette smoke, drawing it into my lungs, it felt like a blessed cleansing relief compared to the filth I had choked on, down in the tunnel. Salvation through self-fumigation.

Many of the other survivors I had spoken to were smoking too, even people who had given up years before were lighting up again. It was a form of self-destructiveness, I thought, and that was because when you felt hopeless and careless, what was the point in worrying about cancer? *We're all going to die. Probably sooner than you think. I should be dead already, anyway. So let's have a fag.*

The flashbacks were not like a documentary excerpt, but a series of fragmented memories of powerful physical feelings; the fierce heat of the air pushing into my ears, hurting them, the giant force that had smashed me on the back of my head and thrown me to the floor, the sticky carriage floor under my palms, the warm press of bodies around me, the soft squeezing fingers of the hand I had held. The rustle of newspaper pages, dropped by passengers, under my feet, as I stepped through the carriage, the crunch of glass as I walked, the sting in my eyes as they watered from the smoke, the thickness of my tongue, the appalling taste in my mouth. Walking down the tunnel looking at my feet moving over the uneven flagstones between the narrow metal rails, then as the light became clearer, and the tunnel wider, looking at my hand and noticing the small bone of my wrist shining in the dim light looking like the bone of a picked-clean chicken wing; the shock of that, seeing inside my own body, the weight of my forearm on my head where I had tried to stop it bleeding so much by elevating it. It seemed that I had to run and re-run the whole journey through the tunnel over and over again to make sense of all the different flashes of memories. Only then could I start to thread them into a narrative I could follow, so I could understand where I was in relation to the bomb, understand how I fitted into the bigger picture, and let it go. I was a detective, examining the evidence of my shocked senses. But I did not have a professional distance in this forensic investigation.

There was no way to manage these flashback memories, which were so violent and so overwhelming. I was in a state of siege, a prisoner of my own mind. I could not talk about it, because on the few occasions I tried, people looked sympathetic or puzzled, or disbelieving, or even worse, suspicious, as if they thought I was going mad. 'Can't you just stop thinking about it? It can't be good for you to think about it so much,' I was told. But it wasn't that simple. I was desperate not to think about it, but the more I tried not to think about it, the worse it got. I was in a permanent state of high alert, trying to avoid triggers for the memories that were unavoidable.

If I had been caught up in the Boxing Day Asian Tsunami, I could have chosen never to go on a beach holiday ever again. If I had been caught in an avalanche, I could have chosen to avoid mountains for the rest of my life. But how could you avoid crowds, tubes, buses, sirens, young men with rucksacks if you lived and worked in London? In any case, even if I did manage somehow to avoid all these things, it still didn't matter; the oddest things could set the reaction off. Sitting in a hairdressers' shop, I suddenly caught a whiff of scorched hair and a smell of chemicals, and had to rush outside and gasp fresh air as my throat closed with nausea. On a work training day, we had all been given a different coloured balloon, and split into teams. At the end of the morning, the trainer suddenly told everyone to sit on their balloons and burst them; there was a series of loud explosions and I was sprinting out of the conference hall, up the stairs and halfway down the street before I had time to think or explain to anyone. Hot on my heels came Patrick. A few of our colleagues found us ten minutes later, slumped against a wall a safe distance away, me, white-faced, sweating and mortified with embarrassment. They didn't know what to say. Nor did I. Scared of bursting balloons? It was almost funny. Yet my reaction had been to run for my life, and Patrick had known at once why I was running, and instinctively rushed after me to see if I was all right.

I knew what was going on, I knew the name for it. It was a post-traumatic shock reaction, which could develop into full-blown post-traumatic stress disorder in some people. There was no way of telling if you were going to be one of the unlucky ones affected – it could strike down a macho army sergeant but a timid curate might escape unscathed. It could get you however popular or resilient or successful or physically strong or clever you were; it was not a judge of people's personalities or abilities. It could come on relatively soon after the traumatic event, but it could also present many months or years afterwards. Not everyone got it, and being 'shaken up', showing disturbance and shock symptoms, in the first few weeks or months after the event did not mean that you would go on to develop the disorder. PTSD was not a sign of mental illness or inherent instability; instead it was an injury, caused by exposure to an overwhelming threat of death. I remembered the symptoms of traumatic reaction: flashbacks, re-experiencing the event, exaggerated startle responses, hyper-vigilance, insomnia, weight changes, skin breakouts, headaches, flashes of anger, rage, feelings of despair, isolation, powerlessness, numbness, depression, the crushing guilt, the preoccupation with the details of the event. There was the euphoria, anxiety, inability to concentrate, panic attacks, the self-medication with alcohol or drugs, chain-smoking... they were the textbook symptoms, and I realised, grimly, that I could tick almost all of them off the list. And in my case, they had possibly been made worse by the earlier traumatic event being re-triggered by the same body chemicals, and by similar memories of overwhelming stranger-violence being released after the bomb. God knows what other passengers were going through. I wondered if they had even heard of post-traumatic shock or PTSD.

There was still very little widely available information about the condition, and it often went misdiagnosed. There were reports that many sufferers felt isolated and reluctant to come forward in case people thought they were mad, or somehow were failures, or 'weak'. There was a kind of shame and grief involved, and an anger, because after the event, things were not as they had been, and yet it was so hard to explain how they had changed, when there were no visible signs of injury. A series of symptoms could easily be missed even by close family and friends, and the person's behaviour changes put down to their 'being moody' or selfish. I knew sufferers were often told simply to 'pull themselves together'. If they spoke of the haunting thoughts and images that preyed on their minds, they were looked at askance, as if they were obsessive or delusional. Many people had suffered damage to their relationships, lost their jobs or had to change to less well-paid jobs because of having PTSD. And in some cases, it had become fatal: there were people who had committed suicide because they could no longer cope. It was called 'the invisible injury', for good reason. It was the curse of those who walked away alive.

Patrick seemed to be managing okay; fortunately he had been further back in the train, not so near the bomb; nonetheless I was worried about him. He too had been trapped underground, breathing smoke, wondering if he would survive. In his carriage, people had been down there for about forty minutes, crushed together, with no information as to what was going on. Even though he seemed balanced and robust he was only in his early twenties, just starting out in his career; he seemed to me to be very young to cope with all this.

We went back into the training session together, subdued.

After the stomach-churning shock of the police shooting an innocent man, and the fright of the attempted bombings of the public transport system a fortnight after 7th July, I badly wanted to be reassured that we were all safe from bullets and bombs. The news in late July was full of the story of the men who had been filmed fleeing from the tubes and the bus, leaving their fizzing rucksacks on 21st July. The unexploded bombs they had left behind as they fled were analysed forensically, and another unexploded bomb was found dumped in long grass near Wormwood Scrubs. The police investigation proceeded with astonishing speed and the news reported how the police were sure they would catch the men soon. On the last Friday of July I had booked the day off after working flat-out all week on a big pitch. I had intended to relax by tidying up the garden, going for a walk, and avoiding all mention of terrorism and trauma. Instead I sat on the sofa and watched the news compulsively all day, as the police raided a flat in West London. Three of the attempted bombers of 21st July were captured; two of them were filmed on a balcony surrendering on live TV. They did not look like the glamorous terrorists in James Bond movies. As armed police stormed the building where two of them were hiding, they were captured on film by an enterprising neighbour who videoed them standing in their underpants, blinking in the daylight, while police officers shouted instructions at them. The captured men looked almost comical, holding their arms high – one was tubby and ugly, the other just looked like a nerd, a nobody.

I felt giddy with relief, thankful that the police were able to protect us, hopeful – no, sure – that the two attacks in July were connected and that through the capture of the 21st July men, the trail would lead to whoever master-minding and training and funding the bombers. I hoped that the police would find out if there were other bombers, other plots, how many were ready to walk among innocents with hate in their hearts and a bomb on their back. What had looked like a wave of bombings targeting Londoners might stop, I told myself, high with euphoria, and now everything would quickly go back to normal. I wanted it all to be resolved like a stage play, the baddies rounded up and captured, the Mayor announcing that the threat had past, the townsfolk rejoicing, as the curtain falls on the drama.

It worked as a bedtime story for me for one night, and I slept peacefully. But the next day, the fear was back, worse than before, when one of the men who had been arrested, captured in Rome, was reported as having said via his lawyer that he 'didn't know 7/7 was going to happen' and his operation was 'nothing to do with the Pakistanis' (meaning the 7th July bombers, three of whom were Pakistani in origin). He said that he had simply taken the 7th July bombings as a cue to launch his own attempt. Maybe he was lying; maybe he had been misreported. But if it was true, then we were looking at alleged autonomous groups on separate missions.

It all felt too close for comfort: a young man had bombed the train I was taking to work four weeks ago. Then just as I turned away from Warren Street, having decided against getting a tube home, another attempted bomb was set off on a train there, by another man who was, we were told, part of a group of five men, two of whom were apparently living and making bombs in a flat in New Southgate – three miles away from where J and I lived. Another alleged bomber lived in Stoke Newington, which was a mile away. Were there would-be bombers and potential terrorists everywhere? Were J and

I unwittingly living in what right-wing commentators were calling 'Londonistan'? Were the gossiping Algerian men in the coffee shops really GIA guerrillas? Was the cheerful butcher giving me an extra lamb chop in the *halal* butcher really a terrorist-sympathiser? Were we sitting on a powder keg – a clash of civilisations – and would we soon see riots in Blackstock Road and Green Lanes? I began to get the odd hysterical-sounding email and anonymous comments left on my blog, alleging that I was a 'dhimmi fool', a sleepwalking liberal idiot, that I should take sides in the impending race war. I deleted them on sight. The last thing I wanted was to be dragged into some racist far-right paranoid conspiracy theory. I read the news, looking for clues about what was going on.

There was reawakened media interest in Finsbury Park Mosque, a giant red brick building a quarter of a mile away from where J and I lived, and the possible role of the extremist preacher Abu Hamza in radicalising the bombers of 7th July and the alleged failed bombings of 21st July. Abu Hamza, a burly Egyptian who had lost both arms and an eye in an explosion in Afghanistan, was already famous for his regular appearances as a carton villain in British newspapers, waving his hook and coming out with inflammatory sound bites that were quoted gleefully in stories about 'the enemy within'. Abu Hamza was certainly no harmless figure of fun. In 1994, at the time of the opening of Finsbury Park Mosque, he had set up the 'Supporters of Shariah' movement, dedicated to supporting a highly political version of Islam, theology-light but action-heavy. He had railed against corruption, making much of his time abroad in Afghanistan and the theatres of *jihad*, though he had never fought in battle. After visiting Bosnia, he returned to the UK and was given a platform to preach at Luton Mosque. In 1997 he was installed as the main preacher at Finsbury Park Mosque. Initially posing as humble and peaceful, he quickly revealed his agenda. There were complaints from the trustees of the mosque almost immediately, and repeated complaints from concerned members of the congregation about his bullying, rabble-rousing and slurs on the trustees' financial management of the mosque. Despite this, many young people flocked to hear the firebrand 'anti-corruption' preacher and to join his 'Supporters of Shariah' organisation. Compared with the 'greybeard' imams preaching in foreign tongues, his street-smart hi-energy rhetoric apparently had appealed, and his congregations grew quickly. But the content of his speeches soon crossed a line into hardcore extremism, and word began to spread about how he would select recruits for special training, culminating in being sent abroad for training and urged to execute '*jihadi* missions'.

The mosque trustees had tried and tried to remove Abu Hamza from his position of malign influence, and were roughed up and intimidated for their pains. Despite serving Hamza and the mosque occupiers with High Court injunctions and eviction orders, despite Charity Commission investigations and suspensions, despite complaints to the police from members of the congregation and the mosque grandees, he had continued to preach in the mosque. Then, when the mosque closed in 2003 after a police raid in connection with an alleged terrorism plot, he had continued to preach outside the mosque. He had also toured other mosques around the UK, supported by a gang of heavies, preaching hatred and urging Muslims to consider themselves as *jihadi* soldiers, striking back at the enemy *kuffir* – non-Muslims – wherever they were. He had been arrested and questioned on more than one occasion, and in 2003 the Home Office had ordered Abu Hamza to be stripped of his British citizenship. He was arrested and jailed in May 2004 after the US issued an extradition warrant. In October 2004 he was charged with incitement to murder and racial hatred. His trial was to have begun during the week of the 7th July.

Perhaps, the 7/7 bombers wanted to time their bombs to coincide with his trial, as some sick show of support – that though he was imprisoned they would bring his words to life, make them 'meaningful' with spilled blood?

The foreboding I felt didn't feel like an over-reaction to having had a lucky escape. It felt entirely reasonable. But I told myself that it was a trauma reaction and that I had to ignore it. And in any event, if I gave up and never left the house, if I was fearful and lived the rest of my life cringing at the thought of more random violence striking again, the bombers would have won. Even if potential bombers seemed to be everywhere at the moment according to the papers. It was unsettling to think that the part of North London where I lived, the streets I walked to work every day, passing coffee shops and bookshops full of gossiping Algerian youths, were being linked with a man who it was claimed was responsible for recruiting and grooming numerous would-be suicide bombers and at the centre of a global terrorism drive.

But I remembered the evidence of my own eyes: the banner that hung outside Finsbury Park Mosque now proclaiming that 'if someone helps an innocent, it is as if they help the whole world. And if they kill an innocent, it is as if they kill the whole world'. I remembered the concern of my neighbours, the shopkeepers and the taxi drivers, whom I had known and chatted to for years, and I remembered the universal condemnation of 7/7 that I had seen, and I knew that despite the thunderous headlines claiming that that where I lived was a nest of wannabe terrorists, I was not going to be frightened out of enjoying living in Finsbury Park, North London.

Exactly one month after the bombings, on Thursday 4th August, the Piccadilly line reopened. And I decided to take back the journey I should have taken on 7/7. Once again, I put on a new suit, because once again I had a big client meeting. This time, I wore flat shoes, so I could run.

J came with me. I walked the exact same route that I had taken four weeks earlier. It was a bright sunny morning, but cold for the time of year. I bought a ticket, and a newspaper. The station was not at all crowded; on 7th July it had been heaving. There were police officers, with a dog, standing in the ticket hall.

I walked up to a police officer, and said thank you for being there. It felt awkward, but I wanted to acknowledge my feelings of gratitude for what must have been a boring, tiring job standing around trying to protect passengers and make them feel safe. I said I was making the journey on the Piccadilly line for the first time since the bombings, which didn't make sense, because everyone was making the journey for the first time since the bombings. I didn't want to say that I had been on the train when it blew up. But I wanted reassurance.

'Don't worry,' she said. 'There's lots of us here.'

J watched me as I patted the police officer's spaniel.

There are two ways to get onto the southbound Piccadilly line platform at Finsbury Park, depending on whether you want the front or the rear of the train. J started to head left, because he wanted to go on the last carriage. 'No,' I said, pulling at his sleeve. 'I want to go this way.'

I wanted to walk down to the train the same way that I did on 7/7, to take back the exact same journey that I should have had four Thursdays before. It felt very important. So I got on at the first set of double doors. The carriage was almost empty. I sat down, and J sat down, and he read my paper, determinedly normal, and I stared at all the passengers – there were only about eleven of them – and then I stared at the second set of double doors, about ten feet away, where the man with the rucksack had pushed on to blow us all up.

We approached King's Cross. J had to get off there. I kissed him goodbye. As the train doors opened at King's Cross, I remembered all of it. The bang, the smoke, the screams. I looked at the empty seats by the window, and thought of the people who should be filling them. I looked out of the window and saw sombre-faced police. People got on and I looked at all of them. None of them had a rucksack. The doors closed. I shut my eyes, and prayed, silently.

Rest eternal grant unto them, O Lord, and let light perpetual shine upon them. Let light perpetual shine upon them. Amen.

It had been so dark down there.

As the tunnel walls sped past, I saw the cabling on the side had been replaced. I realised that new red wire marked the space where the bomb had exploded and damaged the wires on the sides of the tunnel walls. Over time it would become greasy and black like the rest of the inside of the tunnel. But for now, that flash of red marked a wound.

We made it to Russell Square. The doors opened and people stepped out. I was still there, still safe. I did not have to walk down the tunnel covered in soot and blood and broken glass. I did not have to make my way to the station entrance, leaving the dying, the screaming behind. I did not have to climb up from the tracks to the platform. I could not see the platform properly, because my eyes were full of tears that poured silently down my face.

We got to Holborn, and I could not stop the silent tears falling, because I was still on the train, still making my journey. I put my head in my hands, so people would not see me. We reached Covent Garden and as I got off the train, I looked over my shoulder at the people in carriage one. My eyes were still full of tears, but they had stopped falling. The train set off again, and I watched it disappear into the tunnel, continuing its journey. I wished it well; as it sped away, I sent a prayer for someone to watch over the driver and the passengers and keep them safe from harm. Then I left the platform, and queued for the lift to take me up to street level.

A triumphant feeling rose in me as the lift travelled up to the station ticket hall, and I walked out into a sunny morning. I left the station, turned left and walked down Neal Street, stopping to buy a *Big Issue*.

'How are you?' asked the vendor. I looked him in the eyes, and smiled.

'I'm all right,' I told him. 'I'm fine.'

HAVING ACHIEVED THAT MILESTONE, I felt that it was time for a holiday. Although J and I were both busy at work, and our teams needed us there, it was becoming clear that our professional performances were severely affected by the events of July, because neither of us was sleeping normally or resting during evenings or weekends. I was worried about J, who looked grey-faced and crumpled with exhaustion, black smudges under his eyes. He was taking painkillers most days to manage headaches caused from long days and late nights staring at a computer screen or close reading and drafting of endless legal documents. I had been leaning on him too much of late, and after a year of brutal work pace – he often worked over fifty, even up to seventy hours a week – he had little strength left to carry me. The previous year we had got a cheap deal to Turkey, and this year I judged both of us to be too exhausted to face exploring unfamiliar territory. We managed to get another package deal to the same place.

It wasn't until I arrived and unpacked in the hotel room that I realised the full extent of how terrified I had been in London. The stress caused by my body aching with constant foreboding and shaking with sudden adrenalin surges triggered by news bulletins, travelling on public transport, hearing sirens and seeing crowds began to ebb away.

It was boiling hot, over thirty-six degrees, and I became a sun-drenched sloth devouring novels by the pool under a sky that was a bright, intense blue. My dreams at night were furious, hyper-vivid nonsense; sometimes they were horrifying, but they were never about the tunnel. I woke at dawn every day, but instead of lying in bed biting the inside of my cheek, I would get up and swim in the hotel pool until my shoulders ached. Afterwards I would lie on a towel, letting the morning sun dry me, while little brown birds came up and hopped next to me with their head cocked to one side, looking for crumbs.

J and I spent the hottest hours of the day in the *hammam* (Turkish bath), lying on a warm marble slab and breathing in the eucalyptus-scented steam. Afterwards, a giggling young married couple who worked at the baths would slather us with salty foam, scrubbing away rough skin with a scratchy cloth until we were pink and tingling, sluice us with copper buckets of icy water, and then take us to a room where we could be massaged with oil until the knots in our muscles were kneaded away.

J went to get a shave and a haircut at the Turkish barber, and I observed the procedure warily over the top of my magazine: it involved cut-throat razors, clouds of foam, sweet oil, cotton held between the barber's teeth and threaded across J's forehead to tidy his eyebrows, hot towels, lemon cologne and burning rags patted across his ears. J emerged from under a final hot towel smooth and fragrant and gleaming.

'My God, you look five years younger,' I said in surprise, as the barber's younger brother carefully manoeuvred J's neck with a fearsome cracking noise.

'They really know how to look after men in this country,' J said, beaming.

In the evenings we would smoke a tobacco-free apple-pulp hookah (waterpipe, called *narghile* in Turkish) while the sun set over the mountains and the crescent moon appeared over the shining sea, with the first star next to it, just like the Turkish flag. We ate shrimp, fat olives and creamy feta cheese, drank Turkish beer in tall iced glasses, and sipped apple tea. My skin changed to a dark gold, my hair became lighter and so did my heart. It was good, so good, to be far away from London.

Smoking an apple water pipe or two while the last paragliders floated down from the mountains had become a nightly habit, and over the two weeks we became friends with Master Ahmet, Said, Dimitri, Okan and Hakkan who staffed the waterpipe café on the sea front. After a long evening on the whisky we ended up discussing business, and the night culminated with me designing them a new sign and logo, and J advising on music policy. The café was rechristened 'Ottoman's presents... Café del Mar'. The rebrand worked and there was an immediate, massive upsurge in business. The place became packed out every single night. As a token of their appreciation, Master Ahmet asked J and me if we would like to go on a boat trip around the coast arranged via Oscan, a café patron and friend of his.

The next day was spent basking like a seal colony on the roof of the boat with about twenty other tourists, while the remaining forty or so passengers sunned themselves on the lower deck where there were chairs and tables. The boat chugged across choppy greeny-blue water, stopping regularly so that we could throw ourselves off the roof, snorkel round rocks, and scream as we were surprised by icy underwater springs. All day we were followed, pilot-fish-like by small boats captained by local boys with limited English but huge charm and force of personality, each selling some product or service. The youths would scramble on board our boat whenever we slowed down or stopped, and offer us the opportunity to avail ourselves of various delights. These included cantaloupe melons halved and filled with ice cream (from an electric kitchen fridge lying on its side in a rowing boat); salted pistachios and hazelnuts in twists of newspaper; cheese, chocolate or apple pastries in a basket; and chocolate, honey or banana pancakes, which were made to order by a heavily shawled elderly lady, possibly the grandmother of one of the enterprising young men, with a large hot plate plugged into a generator on a tiny dinghy which bobbed dangerously low in the water. Also on offer were hand and foot massages, or a trip on a jet ski with a local love god.

A teenage girl on our boat took one look and slipped quietly over the side of the boat to be plucked out of the sea and swept off at high speed by a handsome grinning youth while her mother shrieked 'Come back, Alison!'

A minor drama occurred when the boat broke one of its metal ladders on a rock coming into land at Butterfly Valley, the ladders being the means by which we were supposed to enter the water, but this only encouraged the passengers, who were of all ages and sizes, to try wilder and higher leaps and dives off the sides of the boat and the roof. J and I returned in the evening deeply tanned and with feet scratched from climbing rocks, having secured the professed life-long friendship of Kemal, one of the merry Turkish crew who had needed our help in composing a series of romantic text messages to his girlfriend in Ireland. The lovers had met two weeks before; he assured me that they planned to marry as soon as possible. We ended the evening fishing with the captain on his private boat, and drinking Jack Daniel's. We didn't catch a thing.

THE HOLIDAY ENDED, AND IT was back to reality. I went back to work, tense at the thought of taking the tube. After two weeks of complete relaxation, where I had started to feel like myself again and forget the bombs for days at a time, it was hard to return to sirens, crowds, public transport. Once again the insomnia returned as I worried about the journey into work the next day. There was a summer cold going round, and predictably I caught it. Within a few days of getting back from Turkey, my tongue was cracked, my glands swollen, my head pounding and I was unable to breathe through my nose. I gulped water and hot tea and coughed and coughed. I was afraid of why I was coughing, of the oily, poisonous smoke that I had breathed in the tunnel for over half an hour. I had nothing to hold over my mouth and nose and there hadn't seemed any point in trying to protect myself from it at the time. Now I wondered what I had breathed in.

I sent an email round the King's Cross message board to ask if anyone else had respiratory problems, even though I didn't want to think too long and too hard about why it was suddenly difficult to breathe. Other passengers emailed back: many of them had coughs and chest infections too. I had read the reports of forensic workers recovering bodies and wearing masks to protect themselves from the fumes and the risk of asbestos dislodged by the blast. But we had not had any masks. And nobody was sure if we had inhaled asbestos or not. The King's Cross United group messaging system was being used on a daily basis, with people sharing their worries and fears, and encouraging each other, congratulating each other on small triumphs like taking a tube journey for a few stops, or getting an appointment to see an ear specialist about the damage to their eardrums caused by the explosion.

Work was frantic again, and in my lunchtimes I fielded more calls and emails from people who had been on the train and wanted to join the group. It rained and rained, and I worked until eight or nine most nights trying to prepare a presentation and media advertising schedule for a big client. One night, sitting at my desk, I got an email from a man who had lost his friend on the train, asking me to call him. Because he was not family, he said, the police would not give him any details of what had happened to the man he had loved. Yet he badly needed to know.

So I told him. How packed the train had been, how the atmosphere had been almost jolly because of the Olympics news, how people, including his friend, had surged on at King's Cross where the crowd on the platform was six-deep as the trains were all delayed and overcrowded. How the numbers of passengers packed into the carriages, meant that twenty-six had died in a carriage carrying over one hundred people, how they had been the ones closest to the bomb, in the middle of the carriage.

How the doors had closed at King's Cross, how we were all cramped into uncomfortable positions, touching each other because there was no space, and how the train had rumbled off with a hiss and picked up speed as it plunged deeper underground into the tunnel. And then, maybe twenty, not more than thirty seconds or so after the doors had closed, there had been a terrible bang, of huge violence and power. Darkness. Everything stopped.

And I said that I thought that was probably the last thing his friend would have known.

'I saw his hand, his life line,' the man who had lost his friend told me. 'It was so short; I knew his life would be short. I told him. And now I know it was quick. And there was nothing anyone could have done, and nothing he could have done, and nothing he would have known. I hope.'

'Nothing,' I agreed. 'He would have known nothing. That is what I believe.'

Nothing, which is a kind of peace.

Rest in peace, I thought, after I put the phone down. And let us who are left find peace too. Peace be upon all of us. In the name, if you like, of God who is called the Merciful, the Compassionate. Mercy, compassion; these are not bad aims to have, and to call holy. But if they can't be reflected and lived out in human lives, then I would rather have the peace of Nothing, the quietness of darkness.

THE SUMMER COLD TURNED INTO bronchitis and I was signed off work for a few days and given antibiotics. I noticed, as I sat reading the Sunday papers at the end of July, that for the first time since the bombs I had started at the front and read my way through the whole thing without scanning every page for news on 'London bombings', 'King's Cross', 'Victims' or '7/7'. It was a relief to browse the paper like I used to, feeling normal. I realised that grief and fear make you sit at the bottom of a well, wearing blinkers. The world narrows to reflect your own troubled self's concerns.

Everything feels brittle and trite. Work is meaningless, music too painful to hear, socialising leaves you feeling numb or worse, irritated. Everything conspires to lock you into the isolation of preoccupied anxiety. Other people's concerns seem self-indulgent, but so too does your own preoccupation with something no one else can see, no one else can feel. And I felt bad for feeling sad: I'm alive, how much more are others suffering?

It had been easier this time around though. In 2002 I had my own personal tragedy and trauma, but the wider world had known nothing of it. I read, and wrote, and talked and fought my way back out of that one, and it was these tools I had turned to again when the visceral mist of anger and the barrage of PTSD had descended once more. This time I knew the territory and had the tools to hand, bitter though the learning had been before.

But now seven weeks had passed, and the glass walls of the prison felt like they were starting to melt away, the invisible membrane of fear had been torn and the air was coming back in. I was reading the paper again without flinching, I was looking forward to the last party of the summer, London *en fête* for Carnival weekend. The England cricket team were looking like they might win the Ashes, my colleague Warren and I had secured the big pitch we had been working on and the CEO had come down to give us champagne. King's Cross United was becoming a busy little online community and we had organised to go out for drinks on the first Thursday of September. The bank had returned all the money to my account that had been stolen when someone used my cards fraudulently and emptied my account just before I went on holiday.

I was feeling glad to be alive, but in a lazy, contented way, rather than a shuddering, can't-believe-it way. Miff lay at my feet, stretching and rolling, luxuriating in the heat of the sun on her flanks. I knew how she felt. I was smiling again, at the gift I had been given, the return of what I had forgotten: a careless, ordinary day.

CHAPTER ELEVEN

September 2005 – summer ends

W HEN I WAS TWELVE YEARS old, I wrote a list of things that I wanted to do before I died. One of them was to visit New Orleans and to listen to Cajun music while sipping bourbon. As the terrible hurricane headed for the city of music and laughter, I prayed for good luck for New Orleans.

The hurricane hit, the levees broke, the lights went out, and the music and dancing stopped. Hundreds of people were killed and thousands suffered in the aftermath, and received little help. Once more my own small concerns caused me to feel ashamed. I had a safe home, a good job, help and support. My heart went out to the frightened and angry people I saw on the news daily: I read hurricane blogs and gave money to the appeals, like thousands of others, and I fretted. It seemed almost unbelievably shocking that America, the richest country in the world, should be so unable to help its own people. And even televised suffering that made international news was ignored in the bureaucratic chaos and political complacency in the terrible aftermath of the storm.

It was about then that I started to get really angry about politics. The news wasn't just the news. The political was becoming deeply personal. Watching, seeing other people's suffering affected me physically: I couldn't watch people on the television fleeing from bombs, storms, wars, famine, without an ache in my throat and an anger in my chest, hard as a stone. I felt raw and over-sensitised, as if I had lost a layer of skin. This fierce new-found empathy was more than uncomfortable, it was painful. My soft everyday life of work meetings, going to the pub after work, social calls to friends and family, cooking, gardening, dancing, reading, watching films and TV curled on the sofa with J, which had comfortably muffled me before, began to chafe. Perhaps it was yet another manifestation of survivor guilt, the strange phenomenon which haunted those surviving and living when others around them had died or been badly injured. Perhaps the bomb had made me grow up a decade. Whereas the rape attack and the invasion of my body and my home had made me a raging, angry adolescent, hunkering down with my outrage and slamming the barriers up if anyone tried to break through the protective shell, the explosion so near me had left me with an older woman's grief for other people's families, other women's children. Or perhaps feeling sorry for other people, other victims, was the only way I could feel sorry for myself and sidestep the shame of still being here and not having been able to do enough to save others.

I never raged at God. If I thought of God, when I believed

in God, God was as helpless as I was. I saw God as grief-stricken, incapable of intervention. God in the eyes of the Iraqi man turning his agonised face to the camera, holding the body of his child. God in the eyes of the woman screaming and throwing her shawl over her head as the camera panned over her flattened house in Palestine. God in the face of the police officer, running to help the injured outside the suicide-bombed ice-cream parlour in Israel. God in the trudging African refugee families, heading for the desperation of the camps. And God in the blank, shocked faces of the US hurricane victims, paddling in rags through fetid water holding pathetic plastic bags while the President made jokes at a fundraiser far away and the media helicopters chugged overhead. God in the people driving over the state line bringing tinned food and blankets, in the woman placing an arm round her sobbing neighbour and taking her into her house.

It was not God, it was politicians whom I was angry with, the false demi-gods and mighty emperors and swaggering robber-barons of our age, shaping the realities of the world with their policies and initiatives and strategies, making satellite phone calls, while the poor and the ordinary picked up their possessions and their children and fled from the bombs and the soldiers and the tanks and the famines and the storms and the epidemics.

Just as in the months after the rape, I felt over-vulnerable with a new awareness of human frailty learned from being confronted with my own helplessness. But this time, I had been helpless with many other people, and I had found that we could help each other, hold hands in the dark and try to get through it. The anger I had been consumed with after the rape was also back, though there were periods of calmness such as I had found in the garden at the end of August and on holiday in Turkey. The anger, when it came, felt different to the visceral defensive anger of PTSD. Yes, I knew that I had PTSD symptoms again, but this was something new. *Lacrimae rerum*, the tears for the sadness of things. And a new shift in me, an engagement, pulling me towards the problems instead of turning my face safely away.

Coming out of the tunnel of traumatic shock and depression was going to be different this time. I didn't know what I was going to be able to do, in my small way, but I could feel the current moving me and I tried to go with it. Learning from last time, I knew how to use the anger as energy, instead of being flattened by its heavy power, and I knew that if my heart were to recover greenness, I would have to plunge in and get involved.

At the same time, I was increasingly afraid of how I was feeling. I was wary of showing how self-pitying and helpless I felt to readers of my online diary, and afraid to mention my rising political anger in polite society. Perhaps because I was aware of how people had said the original bomb diary had affected them, how they had said it was brave and inspiring, I didn't want to show weakness, didn't want to let them and myself down. And always, always the criticising voice in my head saying shut up, you should be over it, you weren't injured, you haven't lost loved ones, how dare you complain? I didn't want to tell J or my family or my friends how bad it was. So my online diary became my secret therapy. I rationalised it by saying to myself that nobody had to read it if they thought it was self-indulgent claptrap, and it wasn't hurting anyone.

The diary was where I tested the boundaries of my grief and shock, telling a little more each time, watching to see what the reaction was from readers who left comments, feeling exposed, but at the same time calmed. Here was somewhere I could put some of the toxic fear, and as I posted, feel relief. Some people talk to a counsellor, or a priest, or pray to a saint, or to God. I talked to no one and everyone, I let my words run out in a rush and join the billions of words in cyberspace, trusting that it would be safe to do so, that no one would hurt me or condemn me for it. And crossing my fingers that my words, which were prayers and charms and incantations for good luck to return, for the world to be safe again, would be listened to, if not answered.

I STARTED TO GET THE jitters the day before the 7th September. I boarded the tube at Finsbury Park, late again, and once more, it was crowded. More and more people stuffed themselves in as we went down the Piccadilly line. As we approached King's Cross I realised with a thump of adrenaline that I was in the 'wrong' part of the carriage. Not travelling near the front of the carriage where I'd survived, where I had travelled faithfully ever since, but right in the middle, by the second set of sliding doors, where the bomb had been. The doors opened at King's Cross and four young men with big rucksacks began to get on, two Asian, one black, one white. My heartbeat sped up and I swayed, my back and underarms beginning to run with sweat. I could smell the sour reek of my own fear, as more and more passengers followed the young men with rucksacks onto the train, into what I was already thinking of as 'the kill zone'.

I looked at my watch. 8.49am. I couldn't do this. I forced my way off the carriage, pushing against the tide of people. I wanted to apologise, but I was afraid that I was going to be sick. I stumbled to the mainline station, lit a cigarette with shaking hands, and got into the queue for a cab, my mouth dry. At work I was weepy and trembling. I felt ashamed of arriving late and in tears. I hid my face under my hair and worked through lunchtime to make up the time. The next day, and the next, I took a taxi to the office. It was expensive, but work was so busy that I simply could not afford to arrive late, in a state, day after day.

It was a King's Cross United pub session on the Thursday that saved me. The shared camaraderie of fellow passengers and seeing how they were facing their fears meant the crippling terror of the tube receded to manageable proportions again. On the Friday after the KCU pub session, I was back on the tube, with a hangover, travelling early so I could wait for a train that was less full and go right in at the front.

By the weekend I was feeling more normal again. It was Jane's fortieth birthday and she, J and I, my sister, and all of Jane's friends, danced and danced through the night, past dawn, until ten in the morning. People I had known for almost a decade were there. I danced with a kind of wild joy, celebrating life and being alive and surrounded by people I loved with every stamp of my feet and shake of my hips. On the Monday I was back on the tube again. I vowed to keep travelling underground, keep at it as much as I could stand it, for the sake of all my friends, for all the people whom I had never met or spoken to but who had been following my diary and wishing me well. For the sake of myself and my fellow passengers whom I had met. Even if I was afraid, I knew it was better to carry on as if I was not afraid, to keep travelling, and to catch up with friends, and to carry on as normal. It was better to dance than to hide at home, frightened and angry. It's always better to dance, and to hug friends, and to laugh. Take that Al Qaeda, and damn you to the hell of your own imaginings.

But the euphoria of Jane's birthday celebration deserted me, and the determination I had summoned up shrivelled away over the next few days. I had not yet recognised the pattern of a good day, followed by bad ones. Whenever I had a good day I still thought it was all over and I was back to normal again. Then, when the darkness returned I would be anxious and disappointed.

I found myself writing my diary, forcing myself to end each entry on a major, not minor chord, trying to encourage myself, and anyone reading it, to show that light still shines. But things were not sunny. They were darker than grey.

I kept checking in with King's Cross United via the group email system, and there was relief in finding out that I was not alone. The people who had told their friends, bosses, colleagues that they were fine, no really, *just fine*, wrote that they were not sleeping any more. Snapping at people. Suddenly unable to breathe in the middle of the night. There was a wobble in the hopeful equilibrium, and it seemed to hit everyone in the same week, at the same time, as if there were some psychic skein connecting us all. Flies caught in an unseen web, sensing the movement as one or more of us struggled to be free.

And yet the outside world had moved on, and the immediate tasks of day-to-day dealing with stuff connected to 7th July had moved on too. But dammit, now the dark gritty grey had descended, and the bigger picture had become harder to see. I wished that I had seen it coming.

It was not Life and Death anymore. It was no longer the exultation of survival, or the trembling shock of the after-blast. The practical business of scars healing, burst eardrums, wondering what to do about getting to work. It was the slow hard slog of recovery. The taste of things being different. The constant, unwelcome comparison between Before and After, that is held within the self, the private grief for the small lost things.

London was back to how it was before, or at least that was how it looked; the shops were busy, the tubes and buses full, the helicopters and armed police no longer as visible. And more than anything, that was what the King's Cross United people leaving messages said they wanted too.

But it had not quite worked out like that. People's concentration was shot, their sleep disturbed. It seemed that now that the shock had finished reverberating, the insidious damage to the sense of humour, the sense of self was becoming obvious. The cracks were starting to show.

Unfortunately, it seemed that so were the fissures in other people's patience. I hunkered down and used what little concentration I had on getting through my workload in the office without letting the side down. I didn't think I was doing a very good job and I felt bad about it, dreading the meeting I imagined must be coming soon with my boss, the questions as to when I thought I would be functioning normally again. That was a question I still couldn't answer.

I desperately wanted to be the confident, cheerful woman my company had hired in April and who had joined in May. Instead I was an itchy, jumpy, mopey shadow of my former self. My resources were low, I felt flaky, paper-thin and I was frightened of what would happen if I gave into the gnarliness, the greyness, sure that my support system would surely fail. I was fed up with my own company, and unwilling to inflict myself on others. I kept quiet.

It was a case of laying low, and trusting in what I knew from the last time: of telling myself, and writing it down – keep listening to your own breathing, in and out. *Keep putting one foot in front of the other, feel the ground beneath your feet, count the heartbeats. It's always monochrome before the sunrise. This is the greyness that you don't remember when the colours are beautiful. These are the darker times, but it is not full darkness, only darker than grey. The familiar shapes are still there, though you cannot see them. And they will be there in the morning, Rachel, keep the faith. This too will pass.*

I began going out almost every night, because I did not want to think about what was going on and what I was feeling – or not feeling. I accepted an invitation to any social occasion that involved drinking with people. I smiled and smiled, and raised my glass, shrugging off all inquiries as to my general health because I did not want to admit to there being anything wrong, telling people I felt 'lucky'. But I did not feel lucky: I felt cursed. When I was in the house, alone, with J still at work, I found myself slumped and staring into space. Sleeping for hours. One Saturday I spent the whole day asleep, eventually getting up at 5pm, then going back to sleep at 10pm. The following day I slept all of the next morning, and then did nothing all afternoon apart from sit on the sofa and look out the window. I didn't take a shower, or change my clothes from Friday until Monday morning.

I blamed it on yet another cold. But I knew I was becoming depressed. Everything was a massive effort. Going to the shops to buy groceries took me an hour to get started with writing the list, than another hour afterwards to unpack a carrier bag of vegetables. I was either running away from thinking about what was happening by going out and drinking, or sitting on the sofa trying not to think at all, which was even more exhausting. I thought about asking for some counselling, but I couldn't seem to find the energy to ask for help.

At the end of September, I was contacted by a lady called Deirdre who worked for the *Sunday Times*. She told me that she had printed out and read my entire blog – 'all fifty-eight pages of it!' – and that, in her opinion, I could write. Then she asked me to write something for the paper. First of all she suggested I wrote something about compensation. The papers had been discussing the issue of compensation for victims: there had been an outcry over the fact that many seriously injured people had yet to receive any money from the Government's fund for victims of violent crime, the Criminal Injuries Compensation Authority, whereas the charity fund set up by the Mayor of London to accept donations from businesses and members of the public had already started to make payments to victims with very little bureaucracy or fuss. Commentaters in the papers said, and I agreed, that this was not acceptable, that people who were already struggling to deal with life-changing injuries should not be worrying about how they could pay the rent or the mortgage and that the Government should help them, and help them quickly.

I said that I was sorry, but I did not feel comfortable or qualified talking or writing about compensation. I had no experience of asking for it: I had not applied. I was ambiguous about whether I should apply for it at all. 'There are people who have dreadful injuries, people who need full-time medical attention still, people who need proper long-term care and help. I want them to have as much money as they can possibly get.' I pointed out.

All I had was a small ugly scar on my wrist and arm. I didn't mind it: it was my battle scar. When it itched, I felt glad, it reminded me that I am alive, I told Deirdre. I told her that I would be interested in writing about something else, about life after the bombs, about PTSD, the invisible wound. Deirdre suggested that I could write about King's Cross United, the small group of survivors from the train, that she thought readers would be very interested in how passengers were managing, three months on.

I said that I could do that, as long as the group agreed and provided I stayed anonymous. As it turned out, KCU had been discussing how to let more people know that the group existed so that other Piccadilly survivors could find fellow-passengers if they wanted to. I emailed KCU and explained that I had been approached, asked what they thought. Everyone was very positive.

So I wrote the feature, staying late after work and using the office computer, since mine did not have a word-processing program installed. It was very hard to write. Not chewing-the-pencil-can't-think-what-to-say difficult, I mean that it made me cry. It hurt to write. Tears ran off the end of my nose and got into the keyboard and my throat felt as if I had swallowed a pebble. Afterwards, I looked like a boiled owl. But the words flowed almost effortlessly; in that sense it was not hard to write at all. The story told itself.

The first part of the story I had already told, many times. The bang, the terrible screams in the smoke. Then came the part that made me weep, remembering it all. How the frightened people in the train had tried so hard to keep each other calm among the panic. How they had held hands and talked to each other in the dark, in every carriage of the train. Led each other to safety, carried each other, comforted each other. How people united in the darkness of the carriage and tried to help each other, and in doing so, how we had saved ourselves from what would have happened if the horror of the bomb had become the second catastrophe of a panicked stampede.

The second part was how we had emerged into the light and how some of us had found each other, shared our stories. How life was now. How King's Cross United had begun. The small triumphs, the courage people had shown and continued to show. The slow journey towards recovery, the taking back, piece by piece, of what the terrorists tried to take away: sanity, safety, and the ability to travel to work and not be afraid. What a bloody hard relentless slog it all still was.

When it was done, I was glad that I had written it. I sent it around the group email, so people could look at it before it went off to the *Sunday Times*.

Four more people joined King's Cross United in the last week of September. Each of them said what I had said, what everyone had said: *Thank God, I had wanted so much to talk to someone else who was there, someone who understands.*

I badly wanted more people from the train to find out about the group, so they could decide if they wanted to join, consider if it would help them. There were hundreds who were on that train. And I wanted the readers of the *Sunday Times* to understand about post-traumatic shock and PTSD, how it felt to have been part of something terrible, three months on, what it felt like inside, when everything looked like it was getting back to normal from the outside.

People, non-passengers, had shown so much compassion, so many people had said that they wanted to help, but they didn't know what to say. They thought it was best not to mention it. Or that 'you must be okay by now'. They seemed to think that by talking about it, you would become sad, and they didn't want you to be sad. Or they thought that they would feel embarrassed. They thought that they didn't really know what to say in the circumstances.

The thing is, I realised, that people didn't really have to say anything. The greatest service anybody can perform for someone who is shocked, saddened, frightened, hurt, is just to listen. To be there, non-judgementally, and to keep being there. To let the other person be sad, or angry and to not run away or flinch, or try to change the subject, or to jolly them out of it, to give them advice. Just to be with them, in solidarity and sympathy and if necessary, silence. Simple human compassion was enough. And cups of tea.

I dedicated my first ever published piece to my fellow passengers, the people whom I had started a journey with as strangers, a journey that was never finished, that continued still.

SUMMER WAS ENDING. MOST PEOPLE in the office were
back from their holidays and the office was full again.
The days were still warm but the mornings were crisper.
The flowers in the garden looked faded and blowsy. Massive
spiders appeared in the bath and were carefully removed in
my cupped hands before Miff could eat them. Mist settled
over the city at night and the moon grew huge and shone the
colour of amber. Winter boots and suits were displayed in the
shop windows, but office girls still wore their sandals and
summer dresses in the late September heat. People started to
look fed up, though, with their tired summer clothes.

Now September was drawing to a close, I could hardly
remember the optimism I had felt at the start of the summer.
Four months ago, I had left the company I had worked for
after six years. They had been good to me after I was raped,
and so I stayed there, recovered, paid what I felt were my
dues for their support of me after the attack. But it wasn't the
same, I wasn't happy there anymore. I was very successful, I
made them a lot of money, I won awards. But I had lost a lot
of my confidence inside. I put on twenty-five pounds, wore
dark, modest clothes that would not attract attention. I felt
safer as a size 14 woman in black, hair pulled back, makeup minimal. I did not want to attract attention in high heels
and bright colours. I was in mourning for the careless girl
I had been, and I was camouflaging myself to keep myself
safe from further harm, hexing myself against a stranger's
malevolent glance.

In the early spring of 2005, when it felt like it was time
to leave my job, because I had done all I wanted to with my
role and was getting bored, I had become paralysed with self-

doubt. I wondered whether to work in an agency, or a small consultancy, or a big media company, or whether to leave the industry altogether. I couldn't decide, and so I did nothing. I stayed in my job, stagnating, clashing regularly with my boss, working late on pitches I was bored with, coming home and complaining to J who was equally gloomy and who was working endless hours and feeling unappreciated by his firm.

Eventually my frustration at my life passing by energised me to change things. I built back my confidence slowly, week by week, making an effort to look after myself better and lose weight, not to let the rape turn me into a woman forever in *purdah*, to stop punishing myself for what had been done to me by hiding away. It was scary, but what was the alternative? Living like a victim my whole life? I finally made the decision to leave my job, and almost as soon as I did so, I got a phone call from a headhunter. I went for the interview and was offered the job. Not just a sideways move, but a promotion and pay rise, in a firm I had worked for several years before. The company was known for its creativity and energy. My life felt like it was back on track. At last, after three years of low-level depression and bouts of existential despair, the fog had lifted and I was coming out of the tunnel of rape-induced depression and into the light.

I had lost two stone since the start of 2005 by carefully recording what I ate, and exercising more. At the start of the summer I started to paint my toenails crimson again. I co-taught a series of successful dance courses, three times a week – and delighted as the women attending the classes discovered a wild and sexy side of themselves, as we performed for each other, shrieking and clapping and hollering like banshees. J and I planted over forty pots of flowers and crammed them into our little back yard so it became a sanctuary of scent and colour. I began to smile more, even to sing in the shower once again.

J and I pottered about our flat in the evenings and weekends, and we worried about the mysterious leak under the bathroom floor. I went to the theatre, saw my hero Sylvie Guillem dance, astonishingly; I had wanted to see her perform live since I first saw her on TV sixteen years ago. J and I made some new friends. We read the newspapers and watched the news a lot. We drank a lot of cold pink wine. We were invited to four weddings but could get to only one. We talked about getting married ourselves one day. We even discussed children's names.

I started my new job and I loved it. I got on famously with my new colleagues. My confidence and my energy rose and rose. I bought two new suits for work and some more new clothes to fit my slimmer body, which was stronger and more supple from dance classes. I wore bright colours again, rubbed rose-scented oil on my golden skin. I ate sushi, debated politics and the news on internet discussion boards in my spare time, was excited and emboldened by life. I cheered and jumped with my colleagues when we heard the announcement about London hosting the Olympics, watched the amazed celebrations in Trafalgar Square. I celebrated London's successful bid in a pub with my team and my boss. Gin and tonic and cheese and pickle sandwiches all round.

I got on a train the next day, and I thought I was dead for a few seconds as the world exploded, and then I thought that I was blinded. Everything stopped. All was reduced to smoke and an endless scream. The world I lived in, the life I had made fell away, far away, as everything I was became focused on the next breath in, the next breath out, staying alive, escaping from the underworld.

And then everything had started again, but everything was different. Everything shook, exploded and then knitted together differently after 7th July. I knew I was changed now. I told myself that the invisible cracks and scars inside me were where things had joined up together, stronger than before. I tried to wear the unseen tattoo marks with pride. Sometimes they ached, but they were part of me and part of who I was.

Summer had ended, and the world had turned, and the nights were lengthening after the equinox. As the sun cooled, the flowers my love and I had planted began to fade and to die. The air changed to a hazy blue gold in the morning and the spider webs hung shimmering over the geraniums when I went out with the cat and my cup of tea for a few moments of peace before the start of the working day. I was glad that we were leaving the warm days behind. It had started out as a wonderful summer, but the bombs had blown a hole in the joy, laced the hopefulness with fear and foreboding. I hated the bombers for that: 2005 had been the year when everything had finally started to go right again. As the seasons changed, I hoped that I could leave the bad experiences that I now associated with July behind me, and that the year would go back to being a good year again.

'Well, there's good riddance, cat-face,' I said to Miff as I stood in my dressing gown, deadheading the geraniums and throwing the petals into a bucket. 'Welcome autumn. I hope things cheer up a bit from here on.'

CHAPTER TWELVE

Autumn 2005

A S THE WEATHER BECAME COOLER in the mornings, and so less like the experience of going to work in July, the panic attacks became less frequent, but they still came when I wasn't expecting them. I wanted to trust my instincts, but when my instincts told me to smash my way out of the carriage whenever a nervous, sweaty guy got on with a rucksack, I knew my instincts were wrong and had to be forcibly ignored, leading to an internal struggle. I was becoming sick and tired of being sick and scared. It was affecting everything. Every time I thought I was better and over it, it crept in again. J woke up looking anxious the day after I had told him that I had left the train and got to work late because of another thundering, dizzying panic attack. He told me, when I badgered him, that he had dreamt that I had been killed by the bomb. So it was still affecting him too.

At weekends I continued to want to sleep most of the day. J was also lethargic, spending hours lying on the sofa watching sport on the TV. On Sunday 9th October I roused myself and told J I was going to a survivor meeting. Not a King's Cross United pub session; this one had been organised by the 7th July Assistance Centre and the Red Cross. It was to be held in Victoria. I met up with Kirsty, Jane and Emily, three friends from KCU, in a coffee shop beforehand.

Nobody had the address of where the meeting was, so I called the 7th July Assistance Centre to try to get the details. The Centre was set up shortly after the bombings for survivors and families and as a resource for anyone affected by the bombings. Originally it was called the Family Liaison Centre, which had confused me and many other survivors, who thought it was either a morgue or a meeting place only for the bereaved. It had now moved into smaller premises and was doing a good job supporting people with counselling, advice and practical support such as how to fill in forms and find out about employment rights.

I hadn't had a letter about the survivor event, but it had been mentioned to me when I rang the Centre a few weeks ago. Information had also appeared on the KCU message boards. KCU survivors had got into the habit of passing on each and every scrap of official communication received by individuals to the whole group, since it seemed that bureaucracy was chaotic, even months after 7th July, and sometimes people got letters and updates, sometimes they didn't. When I got through to the 7th July Centre, the person I spoke to told me I was not on the list of attendees for the meeting. Apparently my name was missing from the records.

It struck me as ludicrous that I still wasn't on the official list of survivors. On the morning of 7th July I had given the police at University College Hospital all my details, had my photograph taken brandishing my sooty bloodstained bandage and filthy face. I had been interviewed over the phone by the police twenty-four hours after the explosion, spent four hours giving a statement to the police in my garden the weekend after the bombings, visited the Family Liaison Centre in Victoria at the end of July, helped to set up King's Cross United, and called the 7th July helpline several times. And yet apparently I did not exist on their records.

I explained what was going on to Kirsty, Emily and Jane. We had a rant about it over coffee: everything – from registering with the Health Protection Agency (who were apparently meant to be keeping an eye on people who had been exposed to the explosions), to chasing about registering with the NHS Trauma clinic, to finding out that there was a Memorial Service happening and getting seats at it – we had done ourselves, as a group. Survivors seemed to have been reduced to finding things out on the internet, or scanning letters so everyone could read them, passing on numbers, sending round information about PTSD, trying to find out what help was available.

'How many people have fallen through the net?' wondered Jane. We worked it out: there were probably between seven hundred and nine hundred people on the Piccadilly line train that we had been travelling in. Then there were the other trains and the bus, and the passers-by and first responders. About three thousand people, we thought, maybe more. The ones in hospital were getting help, as they absolutely should have been. But the people who had wandered away, like that man whose girlfriend had found him covered in soot and blood in a café, in deep shock, who knew?

'Who the hell is helping them?' asked Emily. 'It makes me so flipping angry. We shouldn't have to do all this shit ourselves.'

'At least we've got an email thing going so we can share what we do know,' I said. 'I suppose if it's in Westminster City Hall we can find out where that is from directory enquiries.'

We caught the Victoria line tube to Victoria. Nobody enjoyed the ride, but as I pointed out, 'What are the chances of us all getting bombed again? Anyway, we all know what to do if it happens.'

'Nobody else does,' said Kirsty. 'There are still no signs on the tubes telling you that if something happens you're basically stuck where you are, because the only way you can get out is via the back of the last carriage or through the driver's door. You can bash at the doors and windows all you like, they won't open if the train gets blown up.'

'You'll have to shout and tell them what to do then Rach, you've got the loudest voice,' said Emily.

And in this way we kept our minds off our fears until we got to Victoria. As soon as we got off the train, we all lit up a cigarette, took a huge drag, and then started laughing at each other because we were all the same: pale-faced and smoking hard, like troopers who had just come out of a battle.

The meeting was on the seventeenth floor of a grim 1960s building called Westminster City Hall.

'That's not exactly ideal for all the people who are scared of lifts,' said Jane. We found a large soulless office room, which had been set up with chairs grouped in four areas, with paper notices saying 'King's Cross', 'Tavistock Square', 'Edgware' and 'Aldgate', and a big central table covered in leaflets about stress. A few people were on crutches. The room would have taken at least sixty people, but there only seemed to be about twenty there.

'If there is a fire alarm', trilled the organiser, after a brief introduction, 'it will be real. So you won't be able to use the lifts.'

I watched people's eyes darken and their faces visibly wince. Oh dear.

There was a buffet. A buffet! That was touching. Like a tea served by kindly ladies in a cricket pavilion. I went with the KCU girls to the King's Cross area, and introduced ourselves, explaining that we knew each other through this email group messaging system that we had set up, called King's Cross United. We explained that we had monthly get-togethers in the pub, and here was the email address if people wanted to come along and meet other Piccadilly line passengers.

We brought our KCU book with the diagram of the train carriages that I had drawn a few months ago. When people first joined the group they always wanted to mark where they had sat or stood, and to look at the names of the passengers near them, so they could share experiences with those who had been strangers on the train, sometimes only voices in the dark. Everyone was very interested in the book and all the people from our train who had come to the meeting in Victoria wanted to sign their names. There were now twenty-three people in King's Cross United, and seven more people waiting to join, who had emailed the group. So that made thirty. Out of maybe nine hundred. Well, it was something.

The King's Cross survivors' corner was by far the most

chatty. We all talked and talked. I recognised a short-haired teenage girl with a composed, sweet face who had been in my carriage. She had been injured, thrown out of the carriage, coming to under a pile of bodies. She told me her age: sixteen. She was very brave and dignified. A Turkish man told me of how he and his son had been on the last carriage. The son had been a student at university in King's Cross. He had not returned to college since 7th July. His mother wept as she talked of her sadness, and her son's isolation.

I gave her the KCU email. 'There are lots of nice girls in the group, maybe he'd like to meet them,' I told her. That made her smile, a little.

Several people I spoke to had not yet returned to full-time work, and most had not used the tube since the bombings. It made me realise how far Jane, Emily, Kirsty and I had come with each other's help. Quite a few people had read my BBC diary. They said it had helped; I was glad of that.

I talked to almost everyone in the room. It was moving and exhausting and afterwards I felt headachy and shaky and sad. And desperately in need of a drink; it was much easier doing these social meetings with other survivors in a pub. We left just after 4pm. I was so glad that the others from KCU were there. The survivor meeting hadn't helped me; I felt drained by it all. But I hoped it had helped other people.

On the train back, we talked about the people we had met and we looked at the book of where they had added their names to show where they had been travelling. As we talked, I suddenly noticed that the whole Victoria line carriage had gone oddly silent. Everyone was listening to us talking unselfconsciously about where we had been in relation to the bomb.

'Maybe we had better shut up, we're terrifying everyone,' I said. We put the book of survivors away, rather guiltily. Jane and Emily got off the tube after hugging goodbye, and Kirsty and I went and had a pint in Finsbury Park. We both agreed that we were pleased that we had made the effort. Kirsty offered to help with the administration of KCU – managing emails from people who wanted to join. Jane and I had met last week, and discussed media strategy and getting the message out to other survivors. KCU had become a good team.

I had been looking forward to a friend's birthday party later. But when I got home my head was pounding with pain, and I was in tears with the sadness of it all, and the responsibility of it, being part of this group who were trying to help each other, of people looking to me to be a leader. I was not a natural leader, or organiser. Running a self-help group was not something I had any idea of how to do. I was muddling though with Jane, Kirsty and Richard, who had been travelling in the first carriage with me, and who had been nearer the bomb. He had been thrown from the train when the doors flew off. He was off work, at home, recovering slowly from his injuries. All four of us were now helping to run the group, having regular discussions about how to help people who felt anxious and traumatised, how to keep the group secure and how to deal with administrative matters, such as the endless media enquiries, but none of us had known each other until this summer. None of us had any training in managing an online group of PTSD sufferers while dealing with PTSD ourselves. Everyone was doing their best, but nobody was exactly at the top of their game right now.

I KNEW WHY I WAS doing this. My faith in the innate goodness of people was being kept alive by the actions of this group of fellow passengers. For every man climbing on a train with a bomb, I now knew there were a hundred men and women who, when that bomb went off, would try to look after each other in the dark. And a thousand more men and women would be hurrying to help. And ten thousand more wishing the victims well, donating money, praying, sending their compassionate thoughts. That was the antidote to hate; that was the kindness and love that broke through anger and fear. That humanitarian reaction – doing something good, just because you could – stood against the nihilism of the bombers, killing innocents, just because they could. That was why KCU, and the actions of people after the bomb had become the light that I lived by, the wellspring of any strength I could muster, my bulwark against the blackness. Otherwise, there was no sense to be made of anything. Why me? Why me, *twice*? Is the world really full of angry strangers who will rape me in my own flat, detonate bombs on my train to work, plot evil in the streets around my home? No, a thousand times no. And if there was anything positive at all I could bring out of these two experiences, the rape and the bombing, then I would grab it with both hands and cherish it and hold onto it. If my experiences of PTSD and recovery could be useful now, then I would share them. If it would help people, help me, I would do anything I could to make it better again.

I had to keep hoping. I had to keep trying. I didn't see what else there was to do.

BY MID-OCTOBER I KNEW THAT I needed a break from all the bombing stuff. I had been running with my choke out for miles and miles and my engine was starting to grind and smoke. But it was not possible to let go, for the King's Cross United group had decided to do a media push to let other survivors know about the group. The timing was important: on 1st November there was to be a Memorial Service for the 7th July victims in St Paul's Cathedral. That meant that the media would be looking to run stories about survivors in the days before the service, which was to be attended by the Queen, the Prime Minister and assorted politicians, faith leaders and dignitaries. Therefore we had a short window of opportunity to get the message out before the news cycle moved on. It was a key time to reach survivors for another reason; we were seeing from the reactions of the group that three months on seemed to be the time for the shock to fade and the impact to really start hitting people, just as the outside world seemed to be of the opinion that you should be 'over it'.

We looked at the media requests that were coming in and we looked at the demographics of the passengers travelling on the tube, so we could work out how best to reach them. I called the company who sold advertising space on the London Underground, and asked for a profile of the type of passenger found on the Piccadilly line at morning rush hour. Then I ran the information through a media software programme at work to check what type of media they read and watched. On the basis of what I found out, and after discussing it with fellow group manager Jane, who also worked in advertising, it was agreed that we would speak to certain newspapers, magazines and TV programmes who had put in requests, by emailing me via my blog. We wanted to talk only to ones that had a good chance of being seen by fellow passengers. So we said yes to BBC local radio, but no to an American newspaper; even though the American newspaper reached many more people, we didn't think anyone from the train would see it. As many people in the group were wary of interviews being conducted by journalists, and said they would prefer to talk to someone who was there, I agreed to write two articles – one for a glossy woman's weekly and the other for the *London Evening Standard*. I offered to give everyone copy approval so that they could be sure that they were not misquoted, and to pass the article round the whole group so we could all be sure it was okay. Other members of the group did interviews too. Richard gave a radio interview to Frank Gardner, the BBC's Security correspondent. Frank had lost the use of his legs after a terror attack some years before. Frank also spoke to Gill Hicks, who had lost both her legs in the explosion. The interview was almost unbearably moving.

Writing as a journalist about people's worst experiences was very hard, especially as I was not trained as a journalist. Telling my own story was one thing; telling other people's stories was a big responsibility. Writing it all up, after work or at the weekend, forced me to deal with my emotions about the whole thing, because editors demanded emotional viscerality. When I wrote first person accounts, I had to rip my feelings out of their hard shell and bring them into the story. It was hard, particularly as I was finding that the only way I could manage the journey to work and a normal life was to disengage from my feelings about 7th July and try to act as if it had never happened as much of the time as possible. I wondered whether what I was doing was a good thing for my recovery – or not. I noticed that even though there had been journalists and professional writers on the trains, few if any of them had written or spoken about their experiences. What did they know that I didn't about the risks of agreeing to tell and re-live one of the worst moments of your life in the media?

Still, I believed the story should be told and though it was complicated, balancing the demands for a story with the far more important duty of care to the people involved – they weren't 'material', they were people I cared about – I wanted to do it right. I subedited the piece for the woman's magazine, and even though I had spent several hours making sure it read properly, I was surprised to find myself in tears when I read it through for the final time. I still could not believe that this story was my story, our story. Perhaps writing was the way I was managing to cope with it at all, by staying at one remove. Like the war photographer, who records the terrible pornography of violence as an exquisite composition of colour and light behind his camera lens, but whose heart breaks and whose nerve fails after he has put the camera down.

I was caught out crying by the feature's editor who had commissioned the piece. She sounded rattled: when you commission a snappy bomb survivor exclusive you don't usually phone up to find the writer in tears. But then the writer is normally not telling her own story, only someone else's.

The pieces I wrote were well received by King's Cross United members, and by the editors commissioning them. And that same week, the news director of the *Sunday Times News Review* rang me up and asked me to come and have tea with him and discuss further writing. I wondered whether all this was life telling me something: whether I should stop working in advertising and become a writer, if people liked the way I wrote. It was extraordinary, people who wanted to be writers normally worked for years before someone noticed them and commissioned something. Since I had started writing, I had been bombarded with offers.

But all they wanted was bombs, bombs, bombs. I didn't want to write only about bombs; if I was going to be a writer, I wanted to tell many people's stories, not always my own. I was happy to be the person who wrote the stories if people were asking me to, happy to write for the group if people wanted it, for now, but I did not want to be accused of exploiting what had happened to launch a new career. Was being asked to write about the bombs a good thing or not? Were people just after the story, or did they genuinely think I should keep writing, as Fergal Keane and Gary, the BBC editor, had said? It was a minefield, and I recognised that I was in no fit state to make life-changing career decisions. I talked to my parents and to friends, who said that they thought I should keep writing, and who reminded me that all writers use their lives as material, that all writers get noticed somehow, and that what I was doing was not exploitative, since I was being asked to do it. Some people asked, 'What if this is your chance to change your life and become a professional writer, and you miss it, because you are pussy-footing around with all these silly doubts?' Some people said, 'If you are meant to be a writer, you will write, come what may.' J gave me a hug and told me to stop beating myself up about it. Nobody told me to stop, that what I was doing was bad, or wrong.

I decided to wait a while. There was too much to think

about: for now it was a case of getting through the next few weeks, and seeing what happened after that.

ONE OF THE THINGS THAT the bombings had taken away was my ability to listen to music. Since the explosion, I had just about been able to cope with background music in a bar or a restaurant, but unable to sit with concentration and allow myself to feel the beauty of a melody; to be touched by a perfect chord was still too painful. The reason I was distressed about listening to music was because it had the ability to break through the frozen edifice I had constructed, and break me down. To engage with music was to begin the grieving process for what had been lost.

There was one song in the charts that was played again and again over the summer and autumn, by *Coldplay*, called 'Fix You'. The anthemic chorus was 'Lights will guide you home… and I will try to fix you'. The accompanying video showed the singer, Chris Martin, in a tunnel like the one we had walked on 7th July. When I listened to it I thought of all the rescuers hurrying into the tunnel's smoky darkness to rescue the people who were struggling to escape from the train. Those brave people, following their instincts to help, not knowing if they were running towards fire, or a secondary explosion, or a poisonous chemical attack, just running anyway, to find scenes of unimaginable horror. Finding the injured and the dying, and doing their best to 'fix them'.

The song's words made me think of all the tears that had streamed down people's faces since the bombs. Of all those who did not come home. Of those lost ones, who could never be replaced.

It was the one song that almost destroyed me; I was unable to hear it without breaking down. Because it kept coming on the radio at work, several times a day, this reaction I was having to it was becoming a problem, and I was beginning to panic whenever I heard it.

After sending the piece through to the magazine editor, I sat in silence in the study, thinking about the people who had told me their stories. As I sat, the song came through the open window; my neighbour had the radio on and 'Fix You' was playing. Perhaps it was a sign. I decided to stop fighting it, and to listen to the song with my full attention to see if I could get past the effect it had on me. I searched for the song as an MP3 on the internet, found it and made myself listen to it, over and over again. I cried for over an hour until no more tears would come and my face was red and swollen. It was the second time I had cried properly since July.

People kept asking me that autumn how my life had changed after the bombs. Not *if* it had changed, but *how* it had changed. I didn't know if the bombs had permanently changed my life – I hoped not – but there were definitely some differences in my life since 7th July. I was writing, that was the main difference, the permanent change. I wrote what I wanted to read, I did what I wanted someone to do for me.

I didn't want to be alone, shocked, despairing, isolated. I didn't want to think of other people being like that. I remembered how reading about how other people coped had calmed me, helped me, when the world caved in. Hearing their terrible stories meant not being on my own. I remembered what it was like to think that you were going mad, unable to trust your instincts, unable to find your equilibrium, your sense of safety, and I didn't want it to be like that again for me, or for other people. So that was why I started writing on the night of the bomb. Because I believed it would help.

And it had changed my life. But when I thought about it, it wasn't the bomb that had changed my life, it was my reaction to the bomb and other people's reaction to the bomb. After the bomb went off, I allowed my life to change: I had changed myself.

I realised, it doesn't have to be a bomb that changes your life. It doesn't have to be nearly being killed that makes you stop and evaluate how you are, where you are and what you are doing. Assuming you have only one life, and know nothing of whether you will spend eternity with your regrets – why not change? Why not take a chance, write the story, tell that person what you think, speak out?

We all love a happy ending, we all love a redemption, a resurrection, a new beginning. Usually it is very hard to mark the place where the metamorphosis starts. There's no fanfare, no siren, no bombshell. There aren't many occasions in your life when you can look back and say it. Before that day. After that day. My life changed.

Sometimes you can, and even if it breaks you, even if it hurts, it can be a lucky break. You can build your whole new life around before and after the break happened. But mostly you go on changing a bit at a time, a day at a time, so that you and other people don't really notice the change happening.

I think I had already changed before 7th July, but the bomb blew my life apart enough for me to see what was possible, and took away the reasons why I shouldn't, couldn't, mustn't change. It made me stop waiting for something to happen to me.

It made me understand that I was lucky to be alive.

And I lit a cigarette, and tried to be glad about that, instead of crying.

THE PIECE IN THE *EVENING STANDARD* came out, and caused distress when the group saw what had been done. The piece I had written was published unchanged, which was a relief, but the photo had been changed. Instead of us in a pub, the group's image had been cut out and superimposed onto the bombed interior of carriage one. So there we all were, smiling, holding pints, in a murder scene. People were in tears. We had tried really hard to show people that we were just ordinary passengers who met in a pub, and not to sensationalise anything. I felt dreadful about it, after working all weekend to make the story just right, and make sure everyone was happy about entrusting me with their stories. We wrote a letter to the *Evening Standard*, and they wrote back and apologised, saying that they had not meant to cause distress but had meant to make a contrast between these normal-looking men and women, and the terrible hell-scene of the train. They didn't publish the letter or the apology though.

THE CLAMOUR FOR STORIES AND interviews grew more insistent in the days leading up to the official Memorial Service at St Paul's Cathedral, but I did not want to say or write any more. I came back from the service exhausted and feeling ill again, with a cough and swollen glands. There were many bereaved families there, and their grief was palpable, there were rows of VIPs – Tony Blair and Cherie and other members of the Government and the opposition. I sat at the end of a long row with about twenty other people from King's Cross United. Next to me was Jane, who had set up our website. We had our arms round each other. The worst bit was all the cameras and photographers with their zoom lenses. Even though they were in a corner of the cathedral, I was aware of them all the time and I tried to hide my face, feeling exposed. I wanted to take part in the service privately, not to be filmed praying or crying.

As the Queen walked past us down the aisle, close enough to reach out and touch, looking surprisingly small and dainty, with a grave expression, I thought how unreal all this was. Remembering a horrible morning had become a state occasion. It was not politicians or heads of state who had been attacked, but here they stood, in a different part of the cathedral to the ordinary people, whom the terrorists had targeted, to show that the state had been attacked too. The quiet, raw grief of the people directly affected contrasted with the pomp and formalities, and as I watched the Prime Minister leave – by a side door – I wondered whether he prayed for the victims of the bombings, which the terrorists had said were inspired by his foreign policy, or whether he prayed for himself. I wondered why they had not read out the names of the dead.

I wondered whether the Prime Minister would have found it difficult if they had.

The service had helped, the familiar hymns and prayers, the lighting of the candles had a resonance and rhythm that had soothed and calmed me. After the service we went to a pub. There were dozens of people there from the train. The driver of the train was there, the police officer who had been the first on the scene. It was wonderful to be able to thank them and buy them a pint. I kept looking around the busy pub, at the survivors filling the lounge, and saying to Jane and Richard and Kirsty: *Look. Look at us. Look at what has happened. It is awesome.* There were so many new people that I couldn't talk to them all. There were over seventy people now in King's Cross United. All ages, all backgrounds. We decided we needed to have another meeting, a less emotional one, just a night in an Islington bar, no Queen, no Prime Minister, no service, no cameras, no drama. Just talking over a drink and a bowl of chips. Today had been strange, and not ideal for anyone meeting a group for the first time.

The next day there were a few cynical articles saying that the service had granted the bombers publicity and status that they did not merit. But the service was not about the terrorists. It was about trying to commemorate those who had died, and to bring some comfort to those who had lost people they loved, those who were injured, to honour those whose bravery had saved lives, and to show that an attack on one was an attack on all. The cool formality of the service's rituals had a stately beauty, but I wondered whether it had helped the bereaved, or whether it had been just one more agony to endure.

CHAPTER THIRTEEN

Fireworks and politics

IT WAS THE WEEK OF Bonfire Night. The streets of North London were hazed with the smell of explosives and firecrackers and rockets going off with huge bangs all night as local youths made the most of the boxes of fireworks – with names like 'Thunder Lightning Hell Special!' and 'Shock and Awe!' – on sale in the newsagents on Blackstock Road. Normally I loved fireworks, but not this year. I gritted my teeth and turned the TV up loud. The King's Cross United emails pinging regularly into my inbox were full of consternation, as passengers discussed how to avoid the explosions in every neighbourhood that made them jump and shake. I managed to avoid the celebrations on 5th November because I was on duty entertaining clients at a big music awards show they had sponsored. I put on my bling and sipped champagne and counted myself very fortunate to be out of the war zone.

The following night, some pest threw a firework over the wall into the back yard and it exploded just outside the bedroom window as I was asleep. It sounded like a huge bomb. Bang. Flash of blinding light. I leapt out of bed and screamed, and the poor cat peed with fear under the bed. J calmed us both down. I was jangling with adrenalin and anger, and had to be restrained from going outside and looking for the culprit, armed with a cast iron frying pan.

'There must be better ways of celebrating Guy Fawkes' failure to blow up the Houses of Parliament than by selling explosives to teenagers,' I said to J, as I lit joss sticks and sprayed deodorant to get rid of the lingering smell of cat pee. Then I remembered that for the last six years we had cheerfully and irresponsibly set off fireworks in our back garden, once exploding a huge plant pot full of earth by putting a rocket in it upside-down, and I felt like Disgusted of Tunbridge Wells for wanting stricter controls on their sale.

THE GOVERNMENT ANNOUNCED IN NOVEMBER that they were looking to introduce new legislation which meant that anyone suspected of terrorism offences could be locked up – without being charged – for ninety days. I was shocked at this evidence of an increasingly authoritarian tendency, and infuriated by the way that the July bombings were being used to push through draconian laws that damaged ancient rights. What was the point of Tony Blair saying that he wasn't going to let terrorists change our way of life if he then proceeded to change it himself, shredding our liberties and constitution and emotionally blackmailing anyone opposed to the anti-terror legislation by saying that 'the rules of the game have changed'? Britain had coped with bombs before, not only terrorist bombs but with sustained aerial bombardment during the war, which had killed thousands with the weapons of mass destruction of the time. Britain had dealt with organised crime and complex fraud cases, with gangsters and racketeers and dissidents and rebels, for years and years, and it had never resorted to this sort of thing. It had apparently never needed to. Why were home-grown terrorists' bombs more of a threat than an invading Russian or German army? Why was Islamist terrorism worse than Irish Nationalist bombings, or far-right nail-bombing campaigns, or animal rights sabotage, or any of the other threats Britain had faced before?

A FEW WEEKS BEFORE, THEN Home Secretary Charles Clarke had given an interview to the *Daily Telegraph* which was headlined 'When I listen to liberals, I think they're pathetic'. What the hell were they playing at, I wondered? The Magna Carta was not some piece of woolly swinging sixties liberalism. It had been the cornerstone of our constitution for a thousand years.

I had typed a furious entry in my blog in my lunch break.

As everyone reading this knows by now, I was on the bombed train at King's Cross. In the first carriage. So yes, I am not surprised that terrorists seek to do what they can to attack my democratic society, to threaten my liberties, to spread fear, to seek to divide us. I do not expect my democratically elected Government to

227

do the same. I cannot and do not speak for all the victims, and nor can, and nor should Tony Blair and Charles Clarke.

But I know one thing: to defeat terrorism and hate-filled individuals we need to draw strength from each other, to co-operate and talk with each other, whether white or black, Muslim or Christian, Sikh, Hindu, Jew or atheist. Just like we did when the lights went out and the tunnel filled with smoke and we heard the screams of the injured; we drew together, we held hands, we prayed and we did not panic.

I do not see why this ill-thought-out macho posturing, which can only destabilise and divide us, by robbing men and women of the ancient and fundamental right of *habeas corpus*, and by making sections of the community afraid, is going to defeat terror.

And I will not meekly accept that this is to be done in my name. This is panicking, this is fearful, this is not helpful. I expect better than this and I deserve better than this. We all do.

And by the way, calling me a 'pathetic liberal', Mr Home Secretary, is despicable bullying. Terrorists seek to destabilise liberal societies. I am proud to live in one and I will do what I can to protect it by working for harmony, not war, between countries and between faiths, by behaving with confidence and calm, not aggression and machismo. Doing the opposite of looking at people with the suspicion and fear that breeds hatred and mistrust and worse. Taking a bit of damn time to think about things.

Why the rush if not for political gain? How dare you co-opt 'the 7/7 victims' to defend this attack on liberties, as if we are all some amorphous bloodied mass that you can wave in front of the Commons as a fig leaf for your naked desire to be seen to be 'tough on terror'?

I am not going to be a human shield for this Government. Not in my name, I say, you do not act for me. If you want to be tough on terror, then why not be tough on the causes of terror? Why not address, for example, Iraq, why you invaded, the bitter fruits of your ill-thought-out invasion?

And until you do, when I hear your voices dripping sympathy and concern, saying you do this 'for the victims', Tony Blair, Charles Clarke and all the rest of you... I remain disgusted that you should use ordinary people – because that is all we are – bombed people – bloodied people – in this way. Who gave you the right to speak for me, Mr Blair, Mr Clarke? When did I give my blessing to fear-mongering?

You have never asked my opinion. You did not listen when I and a million others took to the streets and you do not listen now.

Bollocks to this. I can't just sit here and take this crap. It's not what I believe in. It's not what I got off the damn train for, frankly.

I FELT BETTER FOR HAVING vented, rattling off the post in less than ten minutes. Within an hour a reader had sent it to the *Times* and it was the lead piece on the *Times* website debate about the issue. Emails started to come in. A man phoned from a BBC radio news desk and asked if I would do an interview, so I nipped out and did so in a five-minute fag break. I stayed anonymous. I seemed to be thinking and saying what many other people were thinking and saying, but the fact that I was a bomb survivor criticising the Government's anti-terror laws made it explosive. I checked and found that I was getting hundreds of hits on my website, some of them from Government IP addresses. The post I had written began ricocheting around the internet as bloggers from across the political spectrum passed it on and linked to it. An anonymous email arrived saying what I had written had been printed out and was being passed around the backbenchers in Parliament! That seemed unlikely but I was pleased that the internet had given me a chance to make my voice heard in a debate that was very important to me, the debate about liberty and security, freedom and fear.

There was, I knew, no reason to take more notice of what I had to say than anyone else's voice, just because I had been close to the terror attacks. And there were probably other terrorism survivors who supported the bill. I had tried hard to make it clear that I spoke only for myself, on my personal web diary. But 'think of the 7/7 victims' seemed to me to be becoming a mantra used by the Government and repeated in some of the press, to defend this unpopular legislation that the Government were attempting to push through. I saw debate stifled by the phrase 'think of the victims'. I saw it as emotional blackmail and thought such tactics had no place in considered law making. How could you make laws based on emotive and controversial news events, without even having a proper debate about it? That was just irresponsible. Hard cases make bad law. Emotive grandstanding makes even worse law. If the laws were reasonable, why bring 'the victims' into it at all? If newspapers and politicians were going to speak about passing laws 'for the victims' without even making contact with the victims, to speak in my name without asking what I or anyone else thought, I would speak my mind back.

And that was how I became a 'political blogger'. It was more empowering than shouting at the television every time the Prime Minister came on.

I was not the only 7/7 survivor to get angry publicly. The *Sun* newspaper used a graphic picture on its front page on the day of the Commons vote on the '90 days' legislation, showing a bloodied, bandaged man with the headline, 'Tell Tony He's Right'. It was desperately cynical. It was also desperately misleading, because the man in the picture, Professor John Tulloch, who'd had the misfortune to sit near Mohammed Siddique Khan as he detonated his bomb on the circle line at Edgware Road, didn't think 'Tony' was right, at all.

Professor Tulloch was not asked by the *Sun* what he thought of Tony's Terror legislation and the '90 days' bill. He wasn't asked if he minded having a huge close-up picture of him all bloodied and shocked on the front page of the UK's biggest-selling newspaper to help to sell the case for the controversial ninety-day internment clause which the Government faced a massive rebellion over. So Professor Tulloch gave an interview to the *Guardian* newspaper the next day, explaining his anger, saying that 'they have given me someone else's voice – Blair's voice'. He said that this was using his image to push through draconian and utterly unnecessary legislation. He said it was incredibly ironic that the *Sun*'s rhetoric is as 'the voice of the people', yet they don't actually ask the people involved, the victims, what they think. He said that, if they had asked to use his image, the words coming out of his mouth would have been 'Not in my name Tony'.

The bill was defeated in the House of Commons. The next day, the *Sun*'s headline screamed 'Traitors!' and named the Labour MPs who had voted against the Government. One of them was my MP, Diane Abbott. I wrote to her and thanked her, and she wrote back, saying she had read the piece I had written.

I was happy to be a 'traitor' with Professor Tulloch and Diane Abbott and many other people. I believed – I will always believe – that democracy is to be cherished and freedom protected. I got quite a lot of emails from other 7/7 survivors and bloggers over the next week, saying they too had been hacked off with the misappropriation of 'in the name of the victims' without consultation. Only one person said that they thought the bill should have been passed, but even they thought there should have been more discussion about it and it seemed a 'knee-jerk' reaction 'playing to the tabloids'.

I went to the pub with King's Cross United that Friday and we had an extremely cheerful evening with lots of wine and bowls of chips. We didn't talk about politics; we talked about hope, and what we wanted from the future, and we congratulated each other on getting this far, commiserated with those who were still too frightened to use the tube, swapped tips for managing panic attacks. Looking around, I was interested to see that we were such a diverse range of people – students and grandparents and office workers, with different religions and backgrounds and politics. It was silly that the media seemed to expect victims to have a collective voice. We didn't all share the same brain because we happened to travel on the same route to work! But we did all seem to share the same, extremely dark, sense of humour.

We talked about whether there would be more terrorist attacks. Almost everyone thought that there would be. I had a bleak conversation with a few people as we speculated about dates. I admitted that I had thought there might be one that day – 11/11 – the day of remembering the dead of the First and Second World Wars. Yet I had still come to the pub, we all had. I said I supposed I would continue to be fearful for a while yet, waiting for the bang and the screams when I stepped into a place crowded with people. But that I accepted that was the price of walking freely after the bomb, it was the blowback of trauma. Which was precisely why the Government shouldn't listen to any sudden demands I might make in a panic to bin *habeas corpus* and change all the laws of the UK and arrest everyone who looked a bit spooky, on the grounds that it might make me feel a bit safer. You can't legislate against hate, and frightening people into making them do what you want them to do never works in the long term. In fact it could work the other way: people would get more radicalised and angry, feel marginalised and oppressed and then they would chafe even more. You would have thought Mr Blair, a Christian, would have remembered the Early Church and the history of the saints and martyrs. All those early Christians tortured to death, mercilessly persecuted by the state – all it had achieved was the worldwide spread of the Christian religion. The gorier the end of the Christian martyrs, the more popular they became, the more they were celebrated in art and music and architecture. If you want to make people feel like martyrs, try driving them underground.

'You'd better not write that in your blog, or the *Sun*'ll be after you. "7/7 Victim Says Bombers Are Martyrs",' said someone, and we laughed, and changed the subject to football.

THE *SUNDAY TIMES NEWS REVIEW* team contacted me again after the piece on King's Cross United had run, and asked me to write some more for them. Bob, the news director, invited me to come and discuss ideas over lunch. He talked about writing 'a big think piece' on the bombings. He said that they wanted a wide-ranging piece on forgiveness and trauma and the aftermath of the bombs, and wondered if I would like to contribute.

At the time of our talking about the feature, fellow-carriage-one passenger Garri Holness, who had lost a leg in the bombings, was in the news again, as the media had discovered that he had a previous conviction for rape that he had sought to conceal. Immediately after the bombings, Garri had been feted for his calmness and his heroism, interviewed in hospital as he had a prosthetic leg fitted. He had become a media 'face of the 7/7 victims', campaigning for better, faster compensation for those affected by terrorism. He had been on the BBC and pictured on the front page of the *News of the World* in the summer, wearing a placard with the words, 'What about the victims?'.

Then a few days later I had walked past a newsagent and seen a big poster for a newspaper reading '7/7 VICTIM'S RAPE SECRET'. For a heart-stopping moment I thought they meant me, and that I was being 'outed' in some way. But no, the press had found out about Garri's past and turned on him. Once he had been a 'hero', now he was a 'monster'.

I felt sorry for him. He had committed a terrible crime, but he had been punished and vilified for it, and he had come out of prison and made a new life for himself. Many years later, he had been swamped by intense media interest, because his leg had been torn off by a terrorist bomb, and he had probably, I thought, been flattered and pleased to be the 'good guy' for once, instead of the bad guy. Then the media had turned on him once more and he had gone into hiding. His building up and his toppling down were a frightening reminder of the power of the press to destroy lives and reputations.

I did not think people should be punished twice for a crime in their past that they had already been judged and imprisoned for, however abhorrent the crime had been. Garri was a teenager in a gang when he had been part of the group that attacked and repeatedly raped two schoolgirls. Now he was a man in his thirties. And now he had lost his leg in a terrible atrocity, and he had been thrust into the spotlight. He had not behaved wisely, in concealing his past from the media, but I did not know how wise I would be if I had been through what he had been through, traumatised and permanently disabled by a terrorist attack.

A taxi driver had mentioned the story which was on the radio when I was travelling to a meeting. 'There's justice for you,' he remarked. 'Couldn't have happened to a nicer guy.'

I tried to say something back, but I couldn't and the taxi ride ended a few moments later. I got through the meeting, on auto pilot, and then stood outside in the street biting my cheek. *Nobody* deserved to be murdered or maimed on 7th July. Saying Garri 'deserved' to lose a leg, that it was 'justice' because he had raped in his teens – what did that imply about all the other people who had been hurt or killed? That they somehow 'deserved' it too? There was no 'justice' in these bombings. It made me angry when people said, 'Everything happens for a reason'. As far as I was concerned, random acts of savagery that destroyed and damaged lives were not preordained, not part of some Destiny or Grand Plan. You might be able to get something positive out of it afterwards, if you survived, and if you did, good on you. But Garri in 2005 was a victim of a crime, just as I was, just as everyone else on that train had been, and he no more 'deserved' to be maimed than I had 'deserved' to be raped in 2002. He had deserved to be jailed for his involvement in the dreadful gang rapes, yes. But after he had paid his debt, his life was his to make his own, for good or ill.

Thinking about all this kept me awake for many nights.

I knew that the papers could find out almost anything that they wanted to about people they had in their sights, just as they had found out about Garri's past. I knew that they were desperate to run stories about '7/7 victims'. (The rebranding of the 7th July explosions in London was an indicator of how the media were now viewing the events as 'the UK's 9/11', though the two events had been very different.)

The media now had me in their sights, as well as Garri, because of the 'Rachel From North London' BBC blog that I had stumbled into writing, which had become my small personal web diary, which had been so therapeutic and which had brought passengers from the Piccadilly train together. I had been on TV only once, the Fergal Keane interview given a week after the bombs. But I had still received enough calls and emails from journalists since 7th July to know that if they wanted to talk to you, they could find you, and they could find out about you. Although every journalist I had spoken to had been polite and pretty considerate, if occasionally clumsy, I had heard tales from other survivors about being pestered by photographers and news crews simply because their picture had become one of the better-known images of the day, and their editors had decided that they wanted a human-interest story follow-up.

One woman had told me how, the day after a picture of herself and her partner, shocked and hugging, had appeared in the global news on 8th July, her house had been besieged by journalists shoving notes through the door and ringing the bell while she was trapped inside. Paul, an ex-fireman who had been passing Edgware Road tube when the bomb went off and who had helped out at the scene, setting up a makeshift triaging system and organising the first aid response, had received endless unwanted attention, and his family and friends had been pestered. Gill, a woman of immense serene grace and good humour who had lost both her legs in the Piccadilly line bomb, told me over dinner of how journalists had tried to get into hospital posing as flower deliverers or members of her family to try and get bedside interviews. It was all scary stuff, and when approached by journalists, my reaction had been to write it myself, to write other passengers' stories at their request and with their full copy approval and amendments incorporated, in order for me and my fellow passengers to try to have some feeling of control and safety when faced by the hungry media beast. The media were going to write stuff anyway, I reasoned, therefore it was better to be part of the process and to ride the tiger rather than be devoured by it.

I had been in the news after the King's Cross United push to tell fellow-passengers of the group's existence. Prior to 7th July, and the *Marie Claire* article being published, I had never been in the news at all. The only time my name had appeared in a newspaper was when I won a £5 book token for being runner-up in the *Church Times* Easter colouring competition when I was eight. The *Marie Claire* piece had been written many months before, but by the strangest of coincidences it had come out the day the bombs struck. The magazine had held back the story until July, because my rape had happened in July, so they viewed it as a 'summer' story.

I had consented to the *Marie Claire* piece because I wanted rape victims to know that justice and healing were possible, to explain about rape trauma syndrome and post-traumatic stress disorder.

I had written about the bomb going off to try to make sense of it, and once more, to try to help others and to help myself by finding common ground and understanding after trauma and tragedy.

None of this had been planned, but like a chain of events, it seemed to have a gathered a momentum of its own. Looking back, it was clear to me where the chain of events had been put in motion. It all stemmed from that decision I had taken as soon as I got out of hospital after the rape. I had lain in a bath looking at all the different injuries on my body, and I had made a promise to myself. *I might not be able to speak now, because my mouth is swollen and my lip stitched and my face unrecognisable, but I will be able to speak soon enough.*

I would not keep silent as the attacker had bade me. I would not be a terrified, broken victim. I would not have my life ruined by this. I would get justice, I would get better, and I would fight back. I would do it with my brain and my words and my actions: all the resources I had against his strength, his thuggery, his threats, his rage and his violence. I would accept and enlist help from every source. I would educate myself about how to survive trauma and I would not go under. And as other people had helped me, so I would try to help other people back. I might be physically weaker than the rapist, and unable to fight him off when he attacked and raped me, but that didn't mean he had won and I had lost. It had become one of the things that defined me, when so many other things about me had dissolved and vanished in the aftermath of the blitz attack, this absolute, non-negotiable refusal to be a victim. Anger was an energy that I could use to focus on getting justice rather than revenge. Outrage was a fire I could use to passionately stoke my arguments and words. Bewilderment could be counteracted by learning everything possible about why this had happened to me. Shame could be thrown back into his face in court when I refused to be ashamed and spoke out, clearly describing to a judge what he had done to me.

And so the fight-back, the self-education, the court case battles and then the victory, the justice at the end. And the healing that it had brought, and the desire to tell other victims the news that I had looked and looked for when it had happened to me: that it could be all right in the end, had led to that *Marie Claire* article, which had been published on 7th July.

Lingering on the platform to read that story meant I missed two trains and got on the one that was bombed. However, it also meant that I stepped further up the train than usual, and stood not in the centre of the first carriage, where the bomb killed twenty-six, but nearer the front, and so was spared serious injury. It also meant that when the bomb went off I was already in a state of high alert, and switched immediately into crisis mode, rather than freezing with shock. My body had unwittingly prepared itself minutes before the bomb, by recalling a violent blow to the head, darkness, choking for breath, a struggle for survival. Though to be in that state was embarrassing on a crowded tube before the bomb went off, it was exactly what I needed to get me through the moments after the explosion.

From what I could see, pondering it now, telling my story had helped to save my life. And now the story was playing out again: rape, bombs, 'victim' or 'survivor'? The choice again of speaking out or staying silent. This time though, the stakes felt higher. Whether I mentioned it or not, I thought it was only a matter of time before the newspapers made the interesting connection that on the same carriage they had a man who had raped and a woman who had been raped. And if they wanted to go into it further, the man who had raped me, the bomber and the man who had lost his leg on the train were all black, and of Jamaican background. I could see this turning into something really nasty, and I wondered what to do about it all, if there was anything I could do to stop this story breaking and becoming another racist, simplistic, pointless media storm. It was inflammatory stuff. And I wondered whether the story would blow up in my face, as it already had for Garri Holness. Perhaps I was over-reacting, over-anxious and wrong in my perception of the media. Maybe they would never find out, or if they did, they would not be interested in running the story. But the appetite for rape stories and 7/7 stories seemed insatiable; and this story had both. I didn't feel safe taking the chance, and then waiting in case it ever came out. Surely it was better to stay one step ahead?

In the end I decided to trust my instincts and to talk to Bob and Mark from the *Sunday Times*, who were commissioning this feature on forgiveness, trauma and the nature of victimhood. I took a deep breath, and explained my back-story to them. The rape, the bomb, my thoughts on the nature of forgiveness that meeting the other passengers and hearing the story of Garri had brought up in me, the weird coincidences behind it all. I said that I was not ashamed or embarrassed about what had happened to me, in fact, I was proud because it had helped me survive. And I said that I was worried about the story coming out the wrong way, and that I would rather tell the story in my own words. *Marie Claire* magazine had not let me write the story myself, even though I had wanted to, even though it had been written in the first person as though I had written it. They had assigned a writer to interview me and put it in their 'house style', and the piece had not really said what I had wanted it to say, though it had still affected me to read it. What did they think? Could that be part of the big 'think piece'? Bob and Mark said yes, it covered all the issues that they were thinking about. They commissioned four thousand words.

I wrote it, all in one night, and the computer crashed, and I lost it. I wrote it all over again and sent it over. Bob edited it, not changing anything but only asking for more details of the rape. ('Sorry, Rachel, the editor thinks it needs it.') I objected, saying it would be too gruesome for the readers. Bob cajoled. In the end I sent over the bald, explicit description I had given in the police statement. I was right; it was too gruesome to publish.

A shoot was arranged in a studio with Francesco, an Italian photographer, who was immensely kind and gentle. The pictures were beautiful. The picture editor of the *Sunday Times* kindly sent me two sets of prints, one for J, and one for my mum.

Rachel North

Bob managed me well; I was no seasoned journalist, just a woman who had started writing a daily diary back in July. I was pleased with the piece when I had finished it and so was Bob. I assumed that they would edit it down to one or maybe two thousand words and that it would run in the middle of the *News Review* as part of a bigger feature. I left Bob worrying about what to title it. Neither of us could think of something that sounded right.

When it came out, it was the main story on the front page of the *News Review*, and it was even trailed on the front page of the main newspaper, with my photo. The piece was simply called 'Rachel's Story' and they had barely edited a word of it. It provoked a big reaction on my blog and on other blogs, and Bob told me that they'd had a great many reader's letters and emails about it. Over a hundred people emailed me to say that it had helped them, that they had been moved, or that they had learned something from it. Men and women of all ages got in touch. An ex-offender, a prison governor, a composer of sacred music, men and women who told me their own stories of rape, police, parents, a probation officer, a psychologist… I would never have thought that my story would garner such a huge reaction. When my rape happened, there had been little news coverage, for grim as it was, such offences took place often enough. But although I felt very vulnerable and exposed afterwards, and especially worried about what my colleagues in the office might say, I was pleased that I had written it. Writing it had helped me, and now I had learned that it had helped others, which made me feel deeply honoured and pleased. Finally, something good had come out of a terrible situation. I dedicated the piece in a heartfelt message on my blog:

To everyone who has ever been a victim of violence, or hate, this is for you. To all the people who have heard me, helped me, comforted and supported me, this is for you. To the men and women of King's Cross United, to DI Dave Hanley, DCI Paul Davidson, DC Ann Brebner and DC Jane Corrigan of the Metropolitan Police Sexual Offences investigation team, Operation Sapphire, this is for you. Thank you for giving me the strength to tell Rachel's Story at last.

O N THE SUNDAY AT THE end of November when the *Sunday Times* piece came out, I had a meeting in the diary. I had met many people from the train over the last few months, and it had been wonderful to hear so many stories of bravery and friendship. To see people who had stood next to each other in the dark greet each other again like old friends was truly moving.

But I had never found anyone who had stood right next to me, until that Sunday, when I finally hugged the girl who had travelled next to me, whose hand I had held, who I talked to in the terrible darkness, who had walked behind me to Russell Square, who had come out of the tunnel with me. I wrote about her in the *Sunday Times* piece without knowing her name, and she had read my diary on the BBC and told her mother, 'that's her, that's the girl I was next to'. She had tracked me down to the urban75 message boards where I had first written about the shattered journey to work, where I had found so much compassion from strangers. She had sent me a message, and we arranged to meet, in Highbury, near where I lived.

I saw her walking towards me on the pavement. Although

we had spent the best part of an hour together, I had not seen her face properly before. We had got separated at Russell Square station, and in any case, we had both been so filthy and blackened as to be unrecognisable with clean faces and tidy hair. We spent the afternoon in a pub talking. She was only twenty-one, a student, studying in Scotland, but during the summer she had a holiday job in London. Her bravery, her sweetness, her hopefulness and grace were inspiring. When I squeezed her hand goodbye I jumped at the familiarity of how it felt. Our experiences had been exactly the same; everything I had written, she had experienced and remembered too. Understanding that we both had the same story and had seen and heard and felt the same things was a very powerful moment and it helped me a great deal to know that my recollection was accurate, and validated by someone who had been at my side.

Some things are too much to carry alone, however strong you think you are. Other voices in the dark can help you carry on, and to continue your journey afterwards.

I had finally spoken with my own voice, and told my own story in my own words, and I was glad of it.

The *Telegraph* ran a piece that weekend about 'Sophie', who was one of the victims of Garri Holness's rape gang. She spoke of how she was no longer a victim, because she worked through a very painful experience and came out the other side. She said that she wanted other rape victims to know that they could, and should, move on. That 'shoving painful stuff in a box doesn't work'.

She said that she had nothing to say to Garri Holness. Reading the interview, I thought there were some similarities to how I felt about the teenager who raped me – I had moved away from him. I was free of him now he was locked up; he was not my problem any more. But if I had seen him pictured in a tabloid newspaper, with a sign saying, 'What About The Victims', as Garri had been pictured when he was campaigning for better, faster compensation for those injured by acts of terrorism, I would have had the angry reaction that Sophie had described when she saw her attacker pictured again, so many years later.

Some things are just too much to take.

I thought that if I met Garri I would treat him the same as any other passenger on my train, and I would talk to him about what happened on carriage one where we had both travelled if he wanted to, but his past was not mine to forgive. I could only talk to him in our shared present as people who took the same train. Months later, I did meet him, at a meeting at the Home Office, and he thanked me for what I had written about him, in the *Sunday Times* and on my blog.

Sophie said in the interview that her life was now 'brilliant'. I was glad about that too. I was glad that she said she did not feel like a victim.

It was too easy to call people victims. The word 'victim', the notion of 'victimhood' hid the real story, the real person. There had been a cross-section of London life on the train Garri and I had travelled on. The man who had raped, the woman who had been raped. The cleaner and the company director. The happy and the unhappy. Men, women, young, old, black, white, Asian, gay, straight, Christian, Jewish, Hindu, Sikh, atheist and agnostic. All of them with complex lives and strengths and weaknesses. Individuals, with their own stories.

I noticed in the months after July, that there were many responses to my writing. I became a cipher, a symbol, a blank screen onto which others projected what they wanted to see, when I wrote about being what was called 'a victim of the London bombings'. Especially as I preserved my anonymity. I had fan mail from libertarians and liberals, from left-wingers, right-wingers, the devout and the god-free. I was co-opted as a Jew and a Christian. I had anonymous incoherent death-threats, and hateful comments left saying I deserved to die for my alleged support of Zionist imperialism (though I had never written about Israel), was told to apologise to the Jews as apparently I and 'my sort' rejoice in suicide bombings in Jerusalem, was vilified and supported on the internet for my perceived support and my perceived lack of support for freedom. Called a traitor and appeaser, called a heroine and an inspiration, called truthful and a liar, a blessing and a bitch.

In the end, of course, I was none of these things. I was, and am, an ordinary woman who got on a train one day to go to work and who found herself one of the people at the centre of a tragic and terrible event that still fascinates the media and many Londoners. I was symbolic only because I could have been anyone. I was known only because, like millions of other people, I had written about it in a blog, trying to make sense of it all. I could have been you. I could have been anyone.

In the end, I am myself. Different from you, but the same. Like the man whom the papers called first a hero, then a villain, I'm neither. He and I are just two of seven million Londoners.

Part of the same city, travelling on the same train.

Seven million Londoners. One London.

CHAPTER FOURTEEN

The ending of the year

KING'S CROSS UNITED HAD A Christmas drinks party in the second week of December. The weeks before, the emails going round had been downbeat: it was hard for many people who were still struggling with PTSD to be happy when they thought of Christmas. Always there was the thought of the people who would be missing round the family table this year. Though nobody in KCU had known any of the people who had died, who had travelled on the train with them, there was still a sense of sadness, and for some, a sense of guilt, that they had been spared while twenty-six others had not. For those feeling fragile, there was the stress of all the running around and organising travel arrangements, buying presents, worrying about money that the festive season entailed, spending leisure time with family members when suffering from exhaustion and depression, not being able to explain why Christmas felt different this year. The 7th July Assistance Centre took lots of calls in the hectic build-up to the holiday season. It was not all gloom though; many people wrote of a sense of deep joy and a new appreciation of their families as they thought of how different Christmas could have been.

But the drinks party, held in the top of a pub in North London, was a jolly affair. The day before the party I had received an unexpected cheque from a newspaper for writing the KCU story, which felt fortuitous. I did not feel right about taking the money myself, so I gave a donation to charity and put the rest of the money behind the bar, telling the group that the newspaper would like to buy KCU a drink. The free bar added greatly to the gaiety of the occasion. It was good to see such a mixed bunch of people screeching with laughter and clapping each other around the shoulders. It was likely that many of us had made the same journey at the same time for years, travelling in the same carriages, with the bored blank-faced routine of the regular commuter, yet had never noticed or spoken to each other. Trapped underground in smoky darkness, all that had changed, and strangers on the train had become friends. You would have thought that we had said all we could possibly say to each other about the explosion by now, and have run out of other things to talk about, so different were we all, but everyone kept swapping places on sofas so they could catch up with yet more people as they came in and by the end of the evening, even the people who had arrived looking sad or stressed looked cheerful.

When the pub closed, J and I and Jane and Eamon from KCU went on to a party at my friend's house and danced in a silly way 'til three in the morning. It was good to let off the head of steam that had built up over the last few months of gloom. There was the sixth-month anniversary to get through, but I felt hopeful that things were getting better for us all.

The next morning, I was woken before dawn by the cat jumping onto the bed in a fright and landing on my head. I was woozy after four hours of sleep and too many vodka tonics, so I detached her claws from my hair on the pillow, stroked her and fell asleep again. I got up a few hours later and went out to buy newspapers and saw a huge black cloud in the North London sky. It was a sunny, freezing day, with a strange light; half the sky looked like a thunderous bruise, the other half, a pale sparkling blue. 'I think it's going to snow,' I said to J. 'It's definitely cold enough,' he agreed, looking at the sky and the strange shadows cast by the black cloud passing before the sun.

There wasn't the clean, ozone smell you get before snow though. The air smelled dirty. I didn't analyse it too much; it was bitterly cold and I hurried inside to make a cup of tea.

Back inside the flat, I took my mug of tea into the study and switched on the computer to read the KCU emails and find out how everyone's hangovers were. One of the group who lived near Hemel Hempstead had been woken up at 6am by a tremendous bang that had shaken the house and rattled the windows. It turned out to be an enormous explosion and fire at an oil depot outside North London. She was 'shaken'. 'I'm not flipping surprised,' came the immediate reply from several passengers.

I checked the *BBC News* website. Hundreds of people had been evacuated. People who lived near to the oil depot had found their doors buckling and their windows cracking. Some people were even blown out of their beds by the force of the blast. There was a story of a security guard who had leapt from a window as the building nearby was devastated by the fire, then watched 200-foot flames 'like we were in hell'. Thankfully nobody was killed, but thirty-six were reported injured in what the news said was the 'biggest non-war-time fire in Europe'. Dozens of 'citizen reporters' took risks to film the spectacle of the devastation and the smoke and the raging fire and send the pictures to the news desks.

J and I went outside to look at the sky. That was the explanation for the dark cloud that filled half the sky, then. No snow would fall, that was all smoke. The explosion had been about twenty miles away. Miff the cat had heard it, and that was why she had jumped onto my head and cried. People who had not been up dancing until dawn also heard it as far away as Norfolk, and even Holland.

A FEW DAYS LATER I met up with one of my best friends, whose mother had died two weeks before. We had been texting a lot, but we had not been able to see each other face to face. We met up at the pub opposite the dance studio where we had been teaching fitness pole dance courses together for the last eighteen months. We had a drink, we talked. Both of us tried not to cry.

Then we did what felt right. We unlocked the empty studio and we danced our asses off. We played the *Rolling Stones* 'Gimme Shelter' and 'You Can't Always Get What You Want', while we warmed up. Then we choreographed a dance to 'Paint It Black'.

Lean, back spin from spiral spin, arch back, touch the floor
Get up, reach up, fireman's spin, sunwheel
Flip over, stand up, plié, shake head
Stand up, walk around the pole, big step, into back spin, twist hips
Egyptian spin, plié...

We danced as hard as we could, moving together, silently, until we were sore and sweating, our breath rising as steam in the cold studio, then we stretched out, and went back to the pub to drink wine. My friend's mother had loved to dance. The slow wasting illness she had suffered from terrified her. She died in her sleep, next to her beloved, on her sixtieth birthday, after having watched a West End show with her family that night. She watched the singing, and the dancing, then she went home and let go. Her two beautiful daughters and her husband had spent the whole evening telling her how much she was loved.

My heart ached for my brave, graceful friend.

After I had kissed and hugged her good night, I got a taxi home, and I stopped at the grocers and talked to my friend the Turkish shopkeeper. I bought milk, cat biscuits, bread. There was a linen basket on the shop floor and inside were some beautiful hand-knitted slipper-socks.

'Are these for sale?' I asked.

The shopkeeper explained that his mother had knitted them, ten, maybe fifteen years before. 'I can't charge you very much, you are a good customer. But I think maybe we should sell them, they are wasted in the house. So I get them out.'

'But the work,' I said. And they were beautiful. Black and white, an Anatolian pattern.

His brother walked in. 'Ma's socks!' he said, looking pleased.

'How much?' I said.

'Um. Five pounds,' said the brother.

'Nooooooo…,' said the shopkeeper, squirming.

'Look at them,' I said, 'they are lovely. And I will always remember your mother when I wear them. And I am happy to pay a fiver, and if you think it is too much you can put some money in the charity box. I think I would like to buy your mother's socks. Mothers are very important.'

'Okay,' said the shopkeeper, and his brother smiled at me.

I wore the socks as soon as I got home. The wool was handspun, tough and soft and very warm, patterned in intricate zig-zags. My feet ached and were cold and cramped after dancing. The socks smelled of lanolin and wool.

They had been made by a mother with love, and my feet could feel it.

IN THE MIDDLE OF DECEMBER, the Government announced that there was to be no public inquiry into the London bombings. Apparently it would 'take too long', be 'too expensive' and 'only tell us things we already know'.

We had spent a thousand days in Iraq and £3.1 billion. Was that too long? Was that too expensive? Was the link between the UK's foreign policy and home-grown radicalisation – which had been realised too late and which the Government still denied – the thing that we already knew? Despite repeated warnings from Muslims, the UK intelligence services seemed for years to have played down the real effects of radical demagogues preaching hate of the state in the UK, who had found a young audience fizzing with a sense of injustice and victimisation, some of whom now supported direct action, rather than peaceful protest. Now hundreds, even thousands of young British men were prepared to fight *jihad*, and to call killing and suicide-bombing, here and abroad, a holy and justified act. What had gone wrong? Was this an embarrassing subject that the Government and security services would rather not air? What of the reaction to the bombings? Were the new authoritarian laws being mooted really what we needed to keep us safe now 'the rules of the game had changed', as Tony Blair informed reporters? Were the changes too little too late – or were they an alarming erosion of ancient liberties – an erosion of freedom as a sop to new fears?

I could not guess the reasons why the Government was refusing to have an inquiry into the worst terrorist attack on English soil, and the first suicide bombing in Europe. They normally had public inquiries into all sorts of things. Surely they understood that the public wanted to understand why it had happened? Surely they knew many people were still interested in the detail of exactly how it had happened and until they knew, would only go on speculating and guessing, which was distressing for those who had been directly affected? Didn't the public, the police, the emergency services, and all the bodies tasked with preparing for and responding to acts of terrorism need to have the opportunity to learn and publicly share the lessons of 7th July, in order to spare suffering and save lives in future? If the terrorism threat was so important that we had to change the constitution and carry ID cards and make draconian new laws, then an independent review of what happened before, during and afterwards, with all the information in one place, conducted by someone independent of the Government with the power to compel witnesses and make recommendations seemed to me not just useful, but downright essential.

A public inquiry would answer the public's questions. Even if the politicians and security services thought it would be inconvenient, or 'take too long', or 'only tell them things they already knew'.

It was the public, after all, who were and who still are the targets, not politicians and spooks. Ordinary people pay the price in blood, in damaged lives, in loved ones not coming home; ordinary people deserve the answers and evidence of lessons having been learned and acted upon.

There are still so many unanswered questions about 7th July. Rumours surfaced that two of the bombers had been known to MI5, had been under surveillance as part of an inquiry into another plot where the alleged plotters had been arrested and were awaiting trial. The 7th July bombers were apparently not 'clean skins', who had struck 'out of the blue', as Charles Clarke, then Home Secretary, had said in the days after the explosions. The security services had been aware of at least two of the bombers; they had listened to them talking and driving around with other suspected terrorists for a few months in 2004, and then they had let them go. Had MI5 dismissed the two men who turned out to be two of the 7th July cell as unimportant, not worth pursuing, and in doing so, made a fatal error? Had they been under-resourced, or simply lacking in imagination? Conspiracy theories were already rife as to what was known about the 7th July bombers and what had been concealed.

And Mohammed Siddique Khan, thought to be the lead bomber, had made the link between his radicalisation and the current foreign policy quite clear in his own words, in his chilling 'martyrdom' posthumous video speech. Of course I agreed that we shouldn't adjust foreign policy out of a fear that disaffected radicalised youths would bomb us in a murderous rage. But denying that there was a link between radicalisation of UK nationals and UK foreign policy seemed mad. After all, the Intelligence and Security Committee had warned Blair before the Iraq war that the invasion of Iraq would increase the threat of terror. If Blair still thought our foreign policy was the right one, I pondered, then he should be able to defend it, and have no fear of questions being asked as to whether it was making us less safe, or why it was making people so angry. It was baffling, it was disappointing, and I could not stop thinking about it.

Why could the public's questions not be answered independently, truthfully, publicly, with dignity and clarity? Even if Mr Blair did not like the questions, did not like the answers, thought he knew the answers already, it was the public, not him, who paid the cost and ran the risks. We had voted his party in, we paid for the wars and the policies to be implemented in our name, we ran the risks on the trains, the buses, the streets each day.

Rachel North

I<small>T WAS ANNOUNCED BY THE</small> Home Office that instead
of an inquiry, there would be a 'narrative' of what had
happened, drawn up by a civil servant. As if we were children
to be placated by a story. I was pretty sure that I already knew
what had happened. I had pieced it together from hearing
dozens of people's first-hand accounts when they joined
KCU, people I had met at survivor events; and I had read all
the newspapers, watched all the news, talked to journalists
who had investigated the story, spoken to police, fire officers
and London Underground staff who had been involved. What
I wanted to know was *why* it had happened, and whether
anything could have been done to stop it happening. I wanted
a debate, and a dialogue instead of denials and draconian law-
passing from the Government. I was fed up, and I decided
that I was not going to shut up about it. I wrote about it and
within an hour one of the blog readers had set up an online
petition asking for an inquiry.

My father phoned me and said he was going to write to
Charles Clarke, who happened to be his local MP. He did
so, using an email-your-MP service. He did not receive an
answer.

I talked to other survivors, and bereaved families, measured
the sense of outrage. Most people seemed to feel similarly
to me. They said they wanted an inquiry, were desperate for
answers to explain 7th July, but there was also cynicism as to
whether anyone would listen, and whether an inquiry would
be a 'whitewash'. But what was the alternative? Just giving up
and going away quietly? I couldn't do that; I felt too strongly
about it, and the more I talked to people who wanted an
inquiry, the more determined I got. I couldn't help the people

who had died and been injured on the train. But I could do this small thing for them and their families. After speaking to people who had lost loved ones, and hearing their grief and anger, I decided to keep at it, until something happened. I had a website, I could campaign from my desk at home, and through the internet. I could get the message out and hear from other people, have the debate about the causes and reaction to 7th July. It wasn't much, but it was something, and I couldn't just sit still and do nothing. Over the next month, and for the next year, I resolved to get busy and to keep pushing, mentioning it whenever there was an opportunity. Other bloggers joined in, including several other 7th July survivor bloggers. The media seemed sympathetic. So what if it took a few years to get there? The Americans had the 9/11 Commission after four years of pressure from survivors and families. I had time, I had my health and energy, which was more than fifty-two innocent people killed by the bombs had. And I knew there was support, because emails and comments kept coming in, from other survivors, bereaved families, and members of the public. I vowed to keep going, as long as it took.

There were more blog-led protests during November. Tim Ireland of Bloggerheads.com, a blogging activist, contacted me to say that he was organising a carol service in Parliament Square, to support free speech and the right to protest. Technically, under the Government's new Serious and Organised Crime and Police Act 2005, section 132, anyone assembling in Parliament Square to protest could be arrested. The draconian law, in the opinion of many, stifled dissent at the heart of our democracy, by imposing a no-protest-without-permission exclusion zone in the square kilometre around Parliament, despite the fact that people had peacefully assembled to voice their opinions outside Parliament for hundreds of years. It was no empty law; members of the public had already been arrested and convicted under the law, among them Maya Anne Evans, a vegan chef, and Milan Rai, a writer and peace activist, for ringing bells by the Cenotaph and reading out some of the names of the soldiers and civilians who had died in the Iraq war. It was widely thought that the law had been brought in primarily to enable the eviction of Brian Haw, a peace protester who had set up a small ramshackle camp with placards and banners outside Parliament and who provided a daily reminder to the PM and MPs of his vociferous opposition to the Government's foreign policy. Due to a loophole in the law, however, Brian Haw was found to be exempt from arrest, as he had been in residence in the exclusion zone since before the law was drafted.

Tim decided to hold an unauthorised carol service in Parliament Square. 'Please note', he emailed, 'that if you attend this carol service it will classify as a demonstration (of faith, hope, joy and/or religious tolerance) and there is a possibility you will be arrested… In this instance, the police have not been notified. They've been invited, certainly, but they have not been notified. We believe that the public has the right to gather in a public place and sing Christmas carols. The police may see things differently, we shall see.'

I hoped that we wouldn't get arrested. I love carols; we had sung them in this country for a thousand years. Even when an Act of Parliament banned Christmas celebrations in 1644, still we sang. Silly laws, and those who make them, don't tend to last long.

The demonstration passed peacefully, with our voices rising in the frosty air as the chimes of Big Ben rang out. The police seemed to be hiding. The media were out in force. Among those interviewed was a human rights lawyer, Mark Schwartz, who was among the singers, who said that the new law was 'vague'. 'Is it compatible with human rights law which is supposed to protect freedom of expression, particularly around Parliament, which is supposed to be the mother of democracy?' he asked.

A police spokeswoman said that they treated the event as a carol service not as a demonstration, so the legislation did not come into play. But it was a demonstration, we all knew that, and we knew we risked arrest for turning up without the right permits, application for which should have been handed in seven days before the demo at a police station in order to get the relevant letter of permission by post.

Perhaps enough people power could change things after all? A small group of people had just proved the Government's harsh new law to be both ineffective and unenforceable. It seemed a positive sign to me.

THAT YEAR, I SPENT CHRISTMAS with J, just the two of us for the first time ever. We were both very tired after the strange year we'd had, and we could not face the roundtrip on public transport to see both sets of J's parents in Preston and Scarborough, his sister in Windsor and my parents in Norfolk. I wrapped presents in the study listening to the Festival of Nine Lessons and Carols from King's College

Cambridge, as my mother always did and her mother before her. We ate oysters on Christmas Eve and watched *Wonderful Life*, curled into each other's arms on the sofa. We were quiet, concentrating on getting the most happiness possible out of each moment. As I cooked Christmas lunch the next day, I thought of all the people I met over the summer who didn't think they'd see Christmas this year. And of those who were missed around the table. Those who would never forget 2005. And I wished everyone what King's Cross United wished me, and each other, a Happy Christmas, and a peaceful New year, and an *ordinary* 2006.

CHAPTER FIFTEEN

Six months on

AS WE APPROACHED THE SIXTH-MONTH anniversary of 7th July – the media interest began to pick up again and I wondered when this story would ever go away. Unlike a private disaster, like the rape, it was hard to get away from reminders of that summer's day. In some ways that made things easier: everyone knew what had happened, because it had been a genuinely shocking event that had made headline news. There was no need to explain all the time. I wondered how hard it must be for other people who have suffered far more, but who had less visible tragedies, to see the '7/7 families and survivors' get so much attention, so much sympathy. There is no hierarchy of pain, media interest does not make the event or the experience more or less valid, but brings with it its own set of problems.

The survivors and families of the Asian Tsunami had been

in the news. For them it was one year on, and there were hundreds of cameras there to record their grief. Surely one of the most intimate, private, painful moments of their lives was captured and beamed around the world, and as a backdrop to their sorrow, the devastation of thousands of villages, hundreds of thousands of lives. A quarter of a million unknown, unphotographed families, lives changed irrevocably by a catastrophe that no human agency can be blamed for.

NEW YEAR'S DAY STARTED WITH me getting into a big row with a lot of conspiracy theorists. Since late summer, there had been a series of odd anonymous messages left on my blog, saying things like, 'FALSE FLAG. INSIDE JOB. SYNTHETIC TERROR.' and 'REMEMBER NORTHWOODS AND GLADIO' and 'SHILL'. I had no idea what they meant, so I deleted them, presuming they were spam. The messages kept coming though. '9/11=INSIDE JOB. 7/7=INSIDE JOB.' Then links to websites, earnest emails urging me to open my eyes and see 'The Truth'. I took a quick look at some of the sites the emails were directing me to; they were full of dire warnings about dreadful deeds carried out by 'The New World Order'. The urban75 message board, where a dim view was generally held of what the site editor called 'conspiraloons' helped to fill me in on the paranoid world of alternative theories circulating the internet. Most of the theories were about 9/11. But now it seemed that '7/7' was starting to spawn dozens of its own conspiracy theories too, and now some conspiracy theorists had discovered my blog and were paying me visits, hoping to convert me to their way of thinking.

In November, I had noticed a lot of traffic coming over from a few websites that seemed to take an extraordinarily sceptical view of the news. I found my original description on the BBC of the bomb going off in my carriage being selectively quoted to endorse a theory that the explosions had not been caused by bombs, but by 'power surges'. Power surges had indeed been thought to be the explanation for the trains ceasing to run on the underground network in the first few moments after the bombs exploded – because those working in the London Underground control rooms saw that the power to the trains running on the Underground system had suddenly stopped. Watching a screen which tracked the progress of the trains running on the network, tube staff did not know that the power had been cut to permit evacuation, or had been lost because of the effects of the explosions. What they saw on their screens looked initially similar to a series of cascading circuit breakers that would result from a major power surge. The National Grid had quickly confirmed, however, that there had been no surge of power that could have caused this, and the first reports that suggested that a power surge in the Underground power grid had caused explosions in power circuits were quickly corrected, once the bombs' devastation was seen, and the survivors had escaped to raise the alarm.

I was therefore surprised to discover that this website, which was linking to mine, was still insisting the 'power surges' story that had been corrected a few hours after the bombs was the true version. It was also claiming that the London bombings were an elaborate cover-up. I followed more links, feeling like

Alice tumbling down the rabbit hole into Wonderland. The victims of 7th July, I read, were not killed by terrorists, instead their deaths were the result of 'corporate manslaughter at the hands of private enterprise'. The site added darkly: 'We've been duped before'. Other theories being pedalled indicated a suspicion of Government contrivance in the bombings, and a repeated denial that four British-born Islamist extremists were to blame. Apparently London Underground should be 'prosecuted for corporate manslaughter', the bus explosion was a fake using 'clever pyrotechnics' and the bus had been filled with 'actors and stuntmen' as part of a 'secret 1000-person terror training exercise' carried out by 'a private company'. The Government had apparently hushed up the tube deaths scandal by linking the two events together – the tube deaths and the exploding bus – and spinning a yarn about 'Muslim bombers' to the complicit media. Never mind the evidence, feel the paranoia.

I read on, following more links. Other sites had similarly wild ideas. Osama bin Laden was a CIA-funded mole who was known as 'Tim Osman'. Al Qaeda was funded by 'The New World Order'. New York's Twin Towers fell on 11th September because they had secretly been packed full of explosives, hidden in the walls (though mysteriously nobody had seen the bomb-planters at work in a building with twenty-four-hour security and office staff in day and night). The World Trade Centre demolition was 'an inside job'. The planes we had all seen hitting the towers were 'holograms'. Or 'pods' carrying missiles; the passengers booked to fly on them had 'been disappeared'. The 'Zionist New World Order', through organisations such as the World Bank, the Bilderberg group and the secretive Illuminati cabal, had invented a Muslim terror threat to lead the world into perma-war and make us all slaves, drones feeding a giant capitalist machine. Everyone had been lied to on a spectacular scale, and like trusting sheep, people were sleepwalking into a dystopian Orwellian future of State-controlled media, State-controlled minds.

All the witness accounts of terrorist atrocities like 9/11 and 7th July, all the suicide-bomber 'martyrdom' videos, all the police and news investigations were 'fakes'. Despite the enormous number of people needed to maintain this massive deception, no whistle-blower had ever spoken out, not one fireman on 9/11, not one construction worker, not one survivor or journalist or emergency services worker in Madrid or London, perhaps for fear of swift and terrible punishment. Yet, despite the tentacle-like global reach of this international coalition of sinister powers, and its ability to control the media, the movies and the mouths of all witnesses, it had a weak point. For some reason it was happy to let armies of self-styled 'truthseekers' expose its evil ways from their bedrooms on home-made websites, without instantly smothering their dissent and bundling them off to reprogramming camps or simply bumping them off. An evil entity happy to kill three thousand of its own people on 9/11 and to kill fifty-two and injure eight hundred on 7/7 was powerless against the mighty forces of bloggers posting their speculations on the internet.

Perhaps it was wise, I thought, that the 'truthseekers' failed to deliver any coherent or credible evidence to support their exciting claims. Otherwise they would surely have been vaporised...

The thing that first puzzled, then irritated, me, as I read

on, was that all of these theories were just that, theories, with little or no evidence presented to back them up. Instead, their authors seemed to delight in poking as many holes into anomalies and minor reported contradictions in reportage as possible. Well, of course there would be inconsistencies in a rolling, multi-sourced news story and ongoing murder investigation, as more information came to light over time. I was happy to leave the more paranoid denizens of cyberspace to their speculations about faked moon landings, CIA-controlled weather and hologram planes hitting a secretly mined World Trade Centre, but I was very angry that they were picking over my personal diary trying to make out that there were no bombs on 7th July. I was also fed up that they were writing to me, and either trying to 'convert' me to their viewpoints or to accuse me of being a Government stooge.

I noticed that many of the 7/7 'Truth Campaigners', while sanctimoniously distancing themselves from the more esoteric theories doing the rounds seemed nonetheless obsessively engaged in a campaign to prove that the Government, police and media were not telling the truth about the events of the day. They were calling for an independent public inquiry, as I was. But the last thing I wanted was for the sane, clear-eyed demands for an inquiry from survivors and bereaved to get muddled up with similar demands from a bunch of people on the internet who seemed to think that the Government might have arranged the bombings for their own unspecified nefarious purposes. And the fact that there were so many inconsistencies and holes in the accounts we had read so far meant that these internet obsessives were going to have a field day speculating away wildly until the cows came home.

Writing on websites that there was no extremist Islamist terrorist threat might be a more comfortable place to stand in than where I was. It enabled people to close their eyes and refuse to face up to the fact that four young British men had been prepared to kill themselves and as many other innocent people as possible, in a criminal act of mass murder, in apparent protest at what our Government was doing in the world. But it was a denial of reality, and a dangerous one at that. It was acting as an apologist for mass murder.

Being publicly and repeatedly referred to on odd websites as a liar and a shill and a fake and a fraud by people I had never met was infuriating and insulting. On one website I had seen a serious discussion as to whether I was really a team of male 'M15 disinformation agents', or a lone 'COINTELPRO' spook (counter-intelligence professional'). 'How much are you getting paid to troll the internet lying to people, Rachel? Wouldn't be surprised if your details led right back to GCHQ,' wrote one poster on a message board.

So on New Year's Day, I wrote a short post on my website, questioning why people wanted to believe this stuff. The replies flooded in, many from sympathetic readers who were equally irritated or outraged by the nonsense on the internet about the bombed bus in Tavistock Square being full of 'actors and stuntmen'. But there were many outraged and angry replies from those who truly believed the conspiracy theories. I tried to argue. But I quickly realised that this was not a logical position, but a belief system that was close to a faith, and impervious to facts, evidence or reason. People Wanted to Believe, and would look for evidence only to support their personal hobby-horse theory. The bombs were 'under the trains', not in them. The CCTV images of the bombers at Luton station were 'Photoshopped' and 'a bad fake'. The eye-witness accounts were 'confused' or 'official propaganda'. Where had the young men – who had been seen with their rucksacks on the security-camera pictures – gone, I wanted to ask. What of their videos explaining and justifying their action, which they had left behind, the DNA evidence of their bodies at the sites, the bombs left in the car, the traces of bomb-making materials at the flat they had been seen going in and out of, which was full of their fingerprints? What of the explosives in their rucksacks that had been found at the scenes? What of the injuries to their bodies that were commensurate with them having been extremely close to the bombs?

Oh, came the answers from the websites, they were dupes, they were patsies, they thought they were involved in a 'secret 1000-man terror rehearsal', they were never in London, they were 'lured onto a fake train in Luton and whacked' [killed], then their body parts placed at the scene by zealous undercover operatives. We can only speculate, I was told, when I asked for a shred of evidence to support any of these theories. *The Powers That Be are hiding the truth, it is not our job to provide answers, or evidence, we can only ask questions because we do not believe their evidence, their official story.*

It was really odd, and very tiresome. Endless questions, on and on, in an endlessly self-referencing conspiracy feedback loop that went nowhere. Some of the theories, some of the theorists seemed quite sensible and many had clearly put a great deal of time and effort into researching their subjects. But they all seemed to have one thing in common, a starting point of deeply cynical disbelief in anything they called 'the official story', and a desire to hunt obsessively for any anomaly, any gap or crevice in the narrative of events into which they could insert the crowbar of scepticism.

The 'July Seventh Truth' campaigners were right, however, on one thing: the bombers had caught an earlier train than was initially reported. The train that the bombers were supposed to have caught had never run. True to form, websites argued that this 'proved' that the 'official' account was a lie (there had not yet been an official account, only stories in the media, sourced from witnesses, police and other sources). '*No CCTV of the bombers in London has ever been shown. Release the evidence!*' chuntered the conspiracy theorists.

They did not seem to want to take into account the fact that the bombers had simply taken an earlier train than the one given out in the police statements. Yet as of writing this in April 2007, CCTV images of the bombers proving they were in London have still not been shown. The conspiracy theories continue to flourish. Perhaps they always will, perhaps there will always be people who prefer fantasy to fact. But an independent inquiry could stop the virus spreading, halt the perfect storm of cynicism and let the truth be widely told, and the lessons surely learned.

I TURNED DOWN ALL THE media requests to do live interviews on the day that marked six months since the bombs had exploded. Instead, King's Cross United gathered for a short ceremony that we had written ourselves. KCU was not a religious or political group, just a self-help group, but we wanted to mark the six months passing with a short period of quietness and reflection. We met at King's Cross station at 3.30pm, carrying flowers and trying to look inconspicuous, fearful of the media. There were about thirty of us, including the driver of the train and his co-driver who had been travelling with him in the driver's cab, who had led us to safety along the tracks with his torch while the driver stayed to help the injured. David, the station manager of Russell Square was there; he had left his post and run into the tunnel, and found the devastation, torn his clothes and taken off his belt to make tourniquets and bandages for those badly hurt. The two British Transport police officers were there, the experienced officer who had heard the explosion at King's Cross and who had run into the tunnel to help, telling his younger colleague to wait on the platform, and if he did not return, to seal the station and report him as missing. And there were the passengers, men and women, some of whom had been injured, all of whom had been frightened, all of whom wanted to remember those on the train who had never finished their journey.

I had spoken earlier in the week to some of the London Underground press officers, and they had agreed to help us organise our ceremony in the middle of a busy train station. I had explained that we wanted to avoid the media, but would like to pay our respects briefly at the King's Cross Piccadilly line platform, the train's last stop before it was bombed as it set off to Russell Square. Where the bomber had boarded the train. At King's Cross mainland station, I met up with Ranesh and Allen, who had briefed the station staff, and they escorted us down the escalator to the Piccadilly line train platform, right to the front, where the bomber had boarded six months before. Even going down the escalator was emotional. Some people in the group had not been back to the Underground, or to the Piccadilly line since the bombing, and they were afraid, and they cried, and others comforted them.

We said the words, taking turns to read the parts of the ceremony.

Leader   We are here today in fellowship, to remember our fellow passengers from the morning of 7th July 2005. We think of them often, especially those who did not finish their journey. We think of all of those who loved them and knew them. We think of the injured, the desolate and those who mourn. We think of the victims of the other London bomb attacks. We think of all those whose lives were changed by the events of 7th July. We think of the victims of all acts of terrorism.

All   **We hold them in our thoughts.**

Leader   We think of those who helped us on that morning, and afterwards, the staff of London Underground, especially the drivers of our train and the staff of Russell Square and King's Cross. We think of the police officers, the fire officers, the ambulance crews and the emergency services, the doctors and nurses and surgeons. We think of the kindness of passers-by and we think of all those who love London and who thought of the people of the city on that day and who held us in their thoughts.

All   **We hold them in our thoughts.**

Leader   We think of our fellow passengers: James Adams, Samantha Badham, Phillip Beer, Anna Brandt, Ciaran Cassidy, Rachelle Chung For Yuen, Elizabeth Daplyn, Arthur Frederick, Karolina Gluck, Gamze Gunoral, Lee Harris, Ojara Ikeagwu, Emily Jenkins, Adrian Johnson, Helen Jones, Susan Levy, Shelley Mather, Mark Matsushita, James Mayes, Behnaz Mozakka, Mihaela Otto, Atique Sharifi, Ihab Slimane, Christian Small, Monika Suchocka, Mala Trivedi.

All   **We hold them in our thoughts.**

Leader   When we all got on that train we did not know that for some of us it would be a last journey and that some of us would not come home. We did not all finish our journey together but we carry you in our hearts. To all that loved you, knew you, worked with you, missed you, our thoughts are with you.

Wherever we travel, we know that we are all fellow passengers and we are with each other on our journey.

WE STOOD IN SILENCE FOR one minute, flanked by London Underground staff who diverted passengers away to the other exit. As we stood, some of the group in tears, a train drew up, and the doors opened. People got off. Then the driver held the train still at the platform, got out of the train, and he too bowed his head, and joined in the silence and prayers.

Kristina – a warm kind-hearted Aussie who had joined the group in the summer and become best friends with Amy, a girl from the carriage behind her – read the last part of the memorial, a short prayer adapted from the gentle service of Compline, at the end of the day.

Leader   Keep watch, dear Lord, with those who work, or watch, or weep, and give your angels charge over those who sleep. Tend the sick, give rest to the weary, bless the dying, soothe the suffering, pity the afflicted, shield the joyous, and all for your love's sake.

All   **Amen.**

Then the train that had stopped drove away, and we went up to the main station, carrying our flowers. We walked to St Pancras church, where people had left flowers on the steps during the week after 7th July, and we met the vicar, whom I had contacted earlier, and he showed us into the church garden, to where there was a statue called 'The Wounded Angel', a calm face hewn in quartz, wings suggested behind, the other half of the profile still unsculpted and so appearing to be shattered and hurt. Here we left our flowers and wreathes. I left twenty-six white roses, one for each person who had died.

We spent a little time in the church, sitting in pews and thinking, or praying. Then I thanked the vicar, and we went to a pub on Euston Road. I felt the release of emotion just above my heart and a lightening as I straightened my back, as if I had just taken off a heavy rucksack. I linked arms with a few of the KCU passengers, and we walked down Euston Road in the pale winter sunshine. Heading for the pub, as usual, buying each other drinks. In the bar I looked at the smiling faces of the KCU men and women around me, and I thought of the glowing, hopeful faces of the people who had died on the train, whose obituaries I had read yesterday as I prepared the ceremony sheets. I was struck by the thought that it could have been any of us.

The bomber had wanted to kill us all, any of us, as many of us as he could. He had not cared when he took that decision to detonate that bomb. And though I have tried and tried, I cannot understand, I cannot imagine what it must have been like to look into the faces of those you were about to kill, to step into the train and to stand right next to them, and to decide. *Now. Now I choose death. I choose self-obliteration. I choose this death, in this tunnel, and I want to cast as many of you people into hell as I can, by killing you with me, for I believe that by doing so, the gates of Paradise will swing open to me, and God will allow me to spend all eternity in a sweet garden of pleasure for doing this in His Name.* This was not an act of God, this was an act of nihilistic, selfish murder, spewing blood and bile and a twisted egotistical projected rage into the face of all that was good. To say that this was done in the name of Allah, the Merciful, the Compassionate was a wicked travesty of an ancient religion. It was the demented, perverted tantrum of a spiteful child, lashing out at others because of his own shame and rage. Those who pedalled this vile ideology, recruited young men to die, telling them falsely that 'there is no drop of liquid more beloved of Allah than blood', were beneath contempt. It was hard not to feel a shattering rage at the thought of all those lives taken, because of such hate, because of such lies, because of such violence from a stranger.

And yet, where did it take you, allowing the rage to consume you and burn you up? Would I not then be the twin of the bomber, with his hate, and his projected fury and his obsession with revenge for the 'wrongs' done to 'his people'? Were we not his people? He had grown up here, among us, not in Iraq or Afghanistan or Palestine, but here, in the UK. He had played sport, been to an English school, listened to music, gone to the cinema, grown up among green trees and paved streets and pubs and fish and chip shops and *Coronation Street* on the TV. He was a stranger, but he was one of us.

Should I therefore give in to despair, fear all strangers, fear all young men, because of the violence I had found at the hands of two young men who were strangers, who had attacked without knowing my name, or the names of anyone they vented their fury on?

No. Because here in this warm, smoky bar was the antidote to despair. Here too were strangers, all ages, all races, all religions, all backgrounds, people I knew only because they had boarded the same train as me six months ago. Because of these people, I could turn my face to the light, and see in any stranger, not a threat, but simply a fellow-passenger on a journey. One man on a train with hate in his heart and a bomb on his back, seeking to divide and kill, versus dozens of passengers drawing together, caring for each other, comforting each other, remembering the dead and injured, celebrating life with new friends.

OUT OF SUCH TERRIBLE DARKNESS, light has come. Out of this tunnel, I stand surrounded by cheer and companionship.

As we said in the pub. 'Take that, terrorists.'

Cheers.

CHAPTER SIXTEEN

Afterwards

I STARTED COGNITIVE BEHAVIOURIAL THERAPY in December 2005, after waiting five months on the list, which was over-subscribed, at the NHS Trauma Clinic in Charlotte Street. Over the next few months, I worked with a therapist to manage my PTSD symptoms, the nightmares, the guilt, the re-experiencing of the explosion and the screams, the depression and the toxic fear. The sense of holding my life together by pulling ragged threads and presenting a bright, brittle face to the world while churning inside, lessened. I had not been 'calm', I had been numb. I hadn't been 'keeping busy', I was manic. I was still on probation in my new role when the bomb exploded behind me and I wasn't 'dealing with it by keeping busy' at work, I had been acting a part of the girl I used to be. Not acting all the time, but enough for it to have an effect, and for the cracks, caused by the strain that at times nearly unbalanced me, to be papered over with cigarettes and alcohol and comfort-eating. Over careful, painful CBT sessions, I learned from the gentle therapist the tips and tricks for managing tube journeys, by concentrating on my breathing, by changing the direction of my thoughts before they flowed into a maze of anxiety and remembered horrors, though I never would accept what she said when she stressed the unlikelihood of it ever happening again.

'Yes it could, and it probably will,' I told her patiently. 'I know it will. The more I find out about what has been going on, the more likely I think it is. Why do you think I keep asking for an inquiry? This threat will go on until some things are changed, and it will take a long, time, and many things need to change. And not just the obvious ones.'

'But it is not likely to happen to you again,' she pointed out.

'It's not very likely that two strangers – teenagers – would randomly almost kill me without knowing my name in the space of less than three years, either, is it?' I said. 'But that's what happened. And I wasn't doing anything risky at the time. I was in my flat, and I was on the way to work. What's that all about?'

We kept working at it, and over time, the nightmares became less frequent, the fear less invasive, though there were still weeks when I would give up on the tube, and pay for a taxi to work. Sometimes I won, sometimes the fear won. Sometimes I was hopeful; sometimes I wanted to give up and give in to self-pity and puzzlement and anger: why me? Why me, *twice*? When I wanted to give up, I would write instead. About how going to work still felt like walking into a war.

About politics, religion, terrorism, the nature of evil. About dancing and cooking and gardening. It was half an hour a day, my writing, but it was the difference between sanity and despair. A small space where I could connect with what I really thought, and say it, because nobody had to read it if they didn't want to. A place to breathe.

Sometimes 7th July was the sad ghost that haunted everything. Sometimes it let me be. I kept faith, because I knew the way out of the tunnel now. I knew that in time the darkness would fade, and spring would come, and my life would come back, changed, but welcomed and more beloved for nearly having been lost.

I was grateful to those who read my words, some of them my family and friends, most of them strangers, who kept the faith with me, who sent me messages of support and who held me in their thoughts. I was more than thankful. I did not have words enough to say how much it helped. I still don't.

IN FEBRUARY 2006, MY LOVE and I went to Amsterdam for my birthday. And in a restaurant in the Old Town, he asked me to be his wife.

'Yes, oh yes,' I said. 'Of course.'

And he gave me a diamond ring, this man I love, who has stood at my side and faced down the storms, and loved me and held me and cherished me, as I have loved him since I met him at a party, danced closer, led him out of the crowd and onto the roof to look at the stars and to sing to him. Who held my hand and told me I was beautiful, when I was beaten and broken and raped and lying on a hospital bed, and who never lost faith in me, whose arms are home and whose hands are gentle, who makes me laugh, who is my companion, my beloved, whose children I want one day to have sitting on our laps. As I write this, my wedding is a few weeks away. A hundred of our friends will be there, including many new friends from King's Cross United. My sister will be my bridesmaid, my brother will read the lesson, and my father and my uncle will take the service in Norwich Cathedral, my mother will be carrying flowers and smiling, and I can't wait.

HERE IS MY LIGHT AT the end of the tunnel; here is my joy and my happiness and my heart's home. Here is a sweetness and a peace, at last, come to me out of the darkness, and I walk into the sunshine and bless it, and hold it, with gladness and gratitude, with all of my thankful heart.

BLESSINGS.